YOGA

IN THE SAME SERIES:

Principles of Aromatherapy
Cathy Hopkins
Principles of Buddhism
Kulananda
Principles of Chinese Medicine
Angela Hicks
Principles of Colonic Irrigation
Jillie Collings
Principles of the Enneagram
Karen Webb
Principles of Fasting
Leon Chaitow
Principles of Feng Shui
Simon Brown
Principles of Hypnotherapy
Vera Peiffer
Principles of Native American Spirituality
Dennis Renault and Timothy Freke
Principles of NLP
Joseph O'Connor and Ian McDermott
Principles of Nutritional Therapy
Linda Lazarides
Principles of Paganism
Vivian Crowley
Principles of your Psychic Potential
David Lawson
Principles of Psychotherapy
Brice Avery
Principles of Reflexology
Nichola Hall
Principles of Self-Healing
David Lawson
Principles of Shiatsu
Chris Jarmey
Principles of Stress Management
Vera Peiffer
Principles of Tarot
Evelyne and Terry Donaldson
Principles of Yoga
Cheryl Isaacson

THORSONS

PRINCIPLES

OF

YOGA

CHERYL ISAACSON

Thorsons
An Imprint of HarperCollins*Publishers*

Thorsons
An Imprint of HarperCollins*Publishers*
77–85 Fulham Palace Road,
Hammersmith, London W6 8JB
1160 Battery Street
San Francisco, California 94111–1213

Published by Thorsons 1996

5 7 9 10 8 6

A catalogue record for this book is available from the British Library

ISBN 0 7225 3212 1

Text illustrations by Anne Chasseaud

Printed and bound in Great Britain by
Caledonian International Book Manufacturing Ltd, Glasgow

The publishers would like to thank Jillie Collings for her suggestion for the title of this series *Principles of ...*

CONTENTS

PART 1

THE IDEAS

1

YOGA AND YOU
AN INTRODUCTION TO YOGA

What do you think of when someone mentions Yoga? People twisting and turning their bodies into strange knotted shapes? Deep relaxation and mind control? Chanting and meditating and staring into candle flames? If so, then you are right on all counts – but you are only seeing part of the whole.

There is an ancient Indian proverb which provides a perfect analogy: three blind men were touching an elephant. The one who was stroking its flank said, 'This animal is very smooth all over, with tough skin and a warm, leathery feel.' Another, standing at the animal's tail, reported: 'It is primarily long and sinuous, constantly thrashing from side to side.' The man who happened to be standing next to the ears of the elephant had a completely different idea. He said, 'This animal consists of thin, fine flaps of skin, velvety soft and highly sensitive.'

All the men were right but none could know the whole picture, which embraced everything they were experiencing from their limited positions, yet was far more. In applying this analogy to our own understanding of yoga, we gain insight into its core principle. We each see the world in very specific ways, defined by our background, education and individual psychology. While having a personal world view might be important in giving us a sense of our own identity, it does not necessarily mean that we are in touch with the whole picture.

Many people today feel that there must be 'something else' to life; another dimension. People call it many different things: a spiritual sense, a connection with a greater power, a higher consciousness, experience of the transcendental, or that somewhat contentious presence — God. That indefinable 'something' may have been lost with the decline of traditional religious practice, or rediscovered through the many alternative systems used by modern seekers; whatever form it takes, it seems to be vital to human satisfaction.

Yoga supplies a complete system of steps by which human beings may work gradually towards this rather elusive level of consciousness. It does this by allowing us to experience, as it were, more and more of the 'elephant hide' of life. Once we feel, know and understand it in all its aspects, we can start to obtain a unified picture of the whole. And it is precisely when we attain that wholeness, that full view of all levels and aspects of life, that we see a chance to leap beyond it. The 'something' that yoga offers could compare to a view of the elephant from a detached vantage point – many faceted, yet entire; in the context of its surroundings and complete. Unified with something more far-reaching than just one small part of the total picture, we become much, much more than just our limited, everyday selves.

This book attempts to show how yoga can work for you. It is a practical guide, because yoga is a practical, life-enhancing science. But it is not just for the person who wants to become fit and supple through doing the well-known physical postures. Primarily, this book seeks to give you a world view of yoga, with an understanding of its history and philosophy, as well as introducing you to the multitude of ways in which it may be applied.

Yoga can affect your whole life and there are many different ways of applying it. It is not supposed to be only for the young and fit, and – most importantly – you can start at any time. Yoga has something for a truly wide range of people, whatever the state of their mind and body. Through using yoga to the full – the intellectual concepts and mental disciplines as much as the physical exercises – you can start to apply it immediately and in a way which works specifically for you. So if you are one of those people who has picked up a yoga book in the past, admired the slim and perfect bodies in the pictures and put it back on the shelf with a sigh, now yoga may be for you after all. This is yoga you can use: a practical way of working physically, mentally and spiritually, so that you get in touch with that which is inside, outside, and in all the spaces in between.

NOT JUST KNOTS

Ever since yoga became popular in the West, the word has become almost synonymous with its physical postures. Bending and stretching, balancing and twisting, the classic body formations of yoga are now a familiar part of the health scene. They appeal to our physically-oriented society, and part of yoga's modern popularity is precisely because it taps into the culture of body fitness.

Undoubtedly physical yoga (usually referred to by its Sanskrit name, *hatha* yoga), is the form towards which most Westerners gravitate. However, this is a comparatively late development in the whole of the yogic tradition, probably dating from around the tenth century AD. Interestingly enough, *hatha* is a particularly difficult form of yoga, designed to harness a whole system of latent energies contained within the body. The object in doing this was so that the body itself would be transformed and become a powerful tool for spiritual enlightenment. Traditionally, the correct practice of *hatha* yoga entailed cleansing and purifying, various forms of breath control, and thousands of postures which acted powerfully upon the basic life forces.

Even when practised in modern conditions, physical yoga still offers many of these aspects. There are very many schools of yoga, some opting for softer forms more suited to untrained Westerners, others concentrating on developing the body's agility and suppleness. Other schools stick as far as possible to the original practices. Most will incorporate some reference to *hatha* yoga's original purposes and teachings.

Hatha yoga must be done with the help of a properly trained teacher, at least initially. It is tempting to try to do too much too soon. Unless you are already a fit person, with good body awareness, yoga injuries can be as common as sports ones. When practised properly, regularly and under guidance, physical yoga can be valuable purely for its stress-busting, strength-building virtues. But anyone who practises long enough will soon find changes taking place which are hard to quantify. Not uncommonly, regular practitioners will begin to notice dramatic improvements in their health, energy and mental state, often becoming calmer and more detached from the niggling worries of daily life. Practitioners report feeling clearer, more directed and more purposeful.

For the person who is not physically-oriented, who finds the exercises of *hatha* yoga too challenging, the full spectrum of yoga offers many alternatives. Other yoga pathways include that of intellectual development, the yoga of service, yoga which uses sound and pattern, and the purely mental discipline of controlling and stilling the variety of thought processes which interfere with our ability to see the world clearly.

THE SOURCE OF PSYCHOLOGICAL FREEDOM

Yoga, then, is primarily a spiritual discipline, evolving from the age-old desire to free ourselves from the mundane human consciousness, designed to help us transcend our limitations and mentally align ourselves with something beyond our own being. For the adept classical practitioner, yoga ultimately provides a way through the complexity of Indian philosophical teachings to a state where one can remain unaffected by life or death.

But what value can all this have for the average Westerner, attracted to yoga because they have heard it can help them relax and give up a few bad habits? How does this grand concept of a unified consciousness relate to the desire to give up smoking or become less stiff in the back? The word 'yoga' is most commonly translated as 'union', so first we should look at the whole idea of what this can mean in modern life. One basic precept here is the formation of a unity within ourselves. Much of the time we go around at war with ourselves, some aspects of ourselves persuading us to go one way, while other parts contradict them in all directions. These conflicting elements may have many origins. They may be instinctive forces of some primitive nature, such as the desire to kill or to defend one's territory. They may have become bred into us, injunctions drip-fed when we were children, part of our basic psychology yet not of our innermost being. Conflicts may be set up, too, of our own making, perhaps as a result of early reactions to events that happened long ago. These could have forced us into defensive attitudes which no longer fit current realities.

Often our activities are not, as we imagine, prompted by free choice, but result from false inner perceptions — the consequence of losing clarity and becoming disconnected with our real, deeper self. Psychology has much to say on this subject, and offers many helpful solutions. Spiritual disciplines such as yoga, however, aim to circumvent the psychological process and shift our basic awareness in order that we can reach unity with our real self without necessarily going through the whys and wherefores of how the 'false' state became so important in the first place.

Therefore when we talk about unity, we can understand one area of it very simply. Forget for a moment about the wider, cosmic implications. Yoga provides us with a way of transcending our own inner state of imperfection. One of the most simple effects of yoga is to create a sense of balance; once we are connected with our internal centre, what we really need will be revealed. Other qualities people can develop through yoga are a growing awareness and sensitivity. Part of the process of becoming out of touch with ourselves is a deadening of feeling. We become conditioned to a kind of numbness, not wanting to know how 'off centre' we really are. Only when we become aware of this distress, this disharmony, can we seek to put ourselves back to rights. By slowing down our normal reactivity, yoga can put us back in touch with our real essence. Although it may feel initially shocking to be shaken out of the comfort zone which has become our 'normality', only then is it possible for us to uncover a deeper reality.

Once this inner harmony starts to grow, detrimental habits become more easily sloughed off. Suddenly in touch with a more real part of yourself, you no longer have the desire to smoke, drink so much alcohol, or eat the things you know are bad for you. So the process of 'giving up' does not become yet another conflict; many yoga practitioners report that the conflict itself disappeared as a deepening connection to their truer self was created.

When it comes to the aches and pains of the physical body,

and finding ways to alleviate them, this process of finding balance and achieving unity is relevant too. Our usual way of coping with physical discomfort is to become accustomed to it and gradually adapt. Such strictures, though, often only accentuate our discomfort. However, creating an awareness of the source of the problem gives us the ability to do something positive about it. Effectively, it gives us control over ourselves and our reactions – and that is the first stage in giving a higher consciousness the upper hand. If the goal of yoga is to transcend normal reality, then a good place to start is precisely with those irritating realities that plague the physical self.

Unity with one's own self has a way of spreading to other relationships. It is often said that what is going on inside a person is reflected in what happens outside them. When we feel bad about ourselves, our relationships with others all seem to be flawed and difficult too. Finding an internal sense of unity is often accompanied by a decrease in family tension and greater harmony with friends. At the same time, yoga's effect of removing you from overpowerful attachment to petty concerns will mean thc ups and downs of relationships seem to lose their reactive hold.

COSMIC REALITIES

So much for internal unity and a more harmonious relationship with the people and things around us. But where, today, is there room for the concept of higher realities, and, apart from in the movies, for the more mystical experiences promised by yoga? The path of the mystic – which, at higher levels, yoga certainly is – has limited appeal to most 'normal' people. Yet many ordinary people, living normal lives, do have experiences which verge on the mystical. How many times, for instance, have you acted on pure intuition and found your instinct to be right; or had so-called 'coincidences' happen which are inexplicable in rational terms; or felt yourself 'knowing' something in an uncanny fashion which seemed to come from nowhere? We may not like to refer to these events in such loaded terms, but as there is little vocabulary for worlds outside our usual consciousness, 'psychic', 'supernatural' or even 'mystical' seems the best we can do.

These unusual experiences are evidence of an expanding consciousness. They often become quite commonplace when we shift the basic foundations of our lives. By leaving our usual preconceptions and suppositions behind we start allowing some other kind of knowledge to work. We may feel we are becoming very intuitive. It becomes easier to see the underlying reality behind situations and people's behaviour. We may pick up unspoken messages, even before others are conscious of them. Some people find they develop healing powers. Although the yoga texts warn against becoming fooled into thinking we are 'spiritually enlightened' on account of these developments, they are encouraging signs that we are tapping into other realities. Fully fledged mystical experiences may not be on our agenda, but it is compelling to open our eyes to the fact that life offers many more possibilities than we ever imagined.

The dictionary definition of a mystic is 'one who believes in spiritual apprehension of truths beyond the understanding.' The supra-rational universe of the mystic has a specific structure and form, which varies in accordance with different mystical traditions. Commonly, the mystical journey is one of ascent though a variety of worlds and their accompanying experiences. These have to do with shedding the ego, or the false personality, with its illusions and attachments. The kind of experiences referred to above are part of the movement of our own consciousness through these different stages. The aim is to reach a state of universal oneness. Although occasionally there are stories of mystics, both ancient and modern, attaining instant enlightenment, a gradual progress is recommended and this is the aim of step by step programmes such as yoga.

Supernormal states of consciousness are always interesting to us. In fact we seem to crave them periodically, indulging in alcohol and drugs in order deliberately to lose touch with our normal state of mind and enter another. What is it about these states that appeals to us? The loosening of inhibitions, the ability to be more honest, feeling more emotionally in touch, freedom from involvement in normal concerns, love for those around us, ecstatic happiness? All of these seem to blossom when we have some help in getting away from normal consciousness, which is why stimulants have, in some shape or form, always been so popular.

The trouble with relying on these expensive ways of getting 'high' is that we are at the mercy of them, rather than the other way round. If we turn to more natural, graduated methods of getting to this state, we control the methods instead of the methods controlling us. We will also develop qualities such as discipline, patience and intelligence, and become more able to guide the way in which we cause a shift of consciousness and gain access to other realities. Rather than the altered state being the temporary result of the substance we have taken, likely to let us down to normal reality with a bump, this state is more likely to stay with us. And, while drugs and other methods can cause us to become dangerously out of touch with normal reality, with yoga we are more likely to remain stable.

This is not intended as a handbook for mystics. But there are ways in which the spiritually inclined person, eager to command his or her own journey into experiences and abilities beyond the normal range, can enjoy what yoga has to offer towards this end. Try it and see!

BECOMING DIFFERENT

Practising any spiritual discipline raises the ultimate question: do people ever change? Can we ever, really, transcend the selves we were born with and raise our consciousness so we become different? The eventual goal of yoga is to cease having all needs and wants, to get rid of the personality, to rise above life as we know it. For how many people is such serious change really necessary? The experience of mystics and sages points to the fact that spiritual bliss is attainable, and that extraordinary peace of mind is possible. For the normal Westerner, such experiences are unlikely and the closest most of us get is perhaps a flash of feeling extraordinarily peaceful and 'at one with the universe'. While this feeling may not last, the fact that it opens us up to a different state of being can itself be life-changing. Much like the change engendered by a near death experience, or a life crisis, these flashes may tell us of dormant powers that exist within us which enable us to reach other levels. Seekers on the spiritual path are actually warned not to strive too hard to reach absolute bliss, because the effort itself breeds desire which mediates against attainment. A gradual, natural process is always recommended.

Unless you are dedicated to the practice of self-mastery, attaining the pure, desire-less state of unity is hardly likely to become a permanent feature of your life. Most of us probably would not want it. What we can hope for, though, are some of the advantages along the way. Peace and tranquillity are rapidly disappearing commodities and most people admit that they long to experience these more frequently. When we drop our concern with mundane things, our consciousness seems to be free to 'look on' without being disturbed, leaving us in a state of calm. These effects of following a spiritual path are well documented and attend the initial stages of detaching from the things of the world.

This state of detachment is worth examining briefly. Detachment has come to have undesirable connotations, suggesting an inability to function in the everyday world, or the necessity of giving up normal feelings for friends and family. Detachment in the yogic sense, however, means leaving an unreal state in order to come closer to a real one which is more spiritually satisfying. Instead of staying at the mercy of emotional responses to people, circumstances and things, you become more adept at keeping in touch with your core reality. You may experience profound feelings, but with a clarity and discernment that has nothing to do with the uncontrollable reactivity more familiar in everyday life. Yogic detachment ultimately means being able to remain equable, whatever the external circumstances.

If you want to change, to achieve a modicum of peace of mind, to extend the boundaries of your consciousness, then this is possible through yoga. The idea, however, is not to alter your character radically, but simply to become 'more oneself'. When the false personality is stripped away, when you can see through your restrictions and constraints and can dispose of them, you will, in a sense, become a new self. No longer bound by the old neuroses and pettinesses, your intrinsic powers will be free to work and it may indeed seem to you and others that you have changed.

Even though it is thousands of years old, yoga can work wonders in present times. Its practice is still constantly evolving, with the emphasis on the physical aspects predominating at the moment. But the ancient advantages, modified to suit our psychology and this age, are very much within reach and needed more today than ever.

2

YOGA IN CONTEXT
YOGA'S HISTORY AND CULTURE

As I explained in the previous chapter, the practices which we term 'yoga' today are just one small, condensed part of what is, in fact, a multifaceted approach to spiritual enlightenment. Forms of these practices can be traced back to 2,500 years ago, while others are said to be medieval. Yoga is also rapidly developing in the modern world. The manner in which it has spread from India over the last one hundred years, especially during the last three or four decades, has meant that it is now, in turn, becoming influenced by Western concepts, which are being incorporated into the tradition in much the same way that yoga has always adapted to the needs of the time.

The fact that yoga is so multifaceted makes it very hard to define. One possible definition is that yoga is a philosophical approach very much connected with fundamental Indian philosophy, consisting of concepts and systems explaining the meaning of life and death, the creation of the universe and the liberation of the soul. It can be – and has been at various times in history – anything from a complete lifestyle to an esoteric cult. At the same time, yoga is a spiritual pathway, offering powerful rituals and meditation techniques which, since time immemorial, have been used to enter other states of consciousness. Additionally, yoga is a system of practical techniques for living life healthily and holistically, from following the correct diet to deep breathing and body strengthening.

Which of these paths are we to follow? Actually, we don't necessarily have to make a choice. The yoga techniques available to most readers of this book are the relatively limited ones, consisting of body postures, or *asanas*, with possibly, depending on which teacher you go to, some breath control and an introduction to the types of mental concentration which can lead into meditation. Some systems of direct meditational teaching are also offered. These are not generally referred to as yoga even though they originate from the same school of thought. However, the yoga which most people expect today is body-oriented, with postural exercises forming a central part. This yoga is a concentrated adaptation of millennia of thought, and will provide what most people want it to – a healthy lifestyle, whether on a physical, mental or spiritual level.

We will take a look now at the diverse process of evolution which has brought us to the yoga we know today. Doing this is not just an academic exercise. In understanding where yoga comes from and how it fits into society, it is possible to gain a sense of its whole nature and purpose.

ANCIENT CULTS, PRIESTS AND SHAMANS – THE YOGIS OF OLD

The people who lived around three thousand years ago in the Indus valley, which spans a huge area from the Arabian Sea to the base of the Himalayas, belonged to one of the earliest known civilizations. The Indus Valley peoples were a peaceful agricultural society, probably with their own priests and ritual magic workers. Terracotta seals have been found dating from this time, which show figures, presumed to be gods, sitting in recognizably yogic postures. The famous lotus pose, with legs folded, hands on the knees and the feet crossed one on top of the other, is classically depicted. These are of great interest to the yoga historian.

In time, the Indus Valley peoples were conquered by Sanskrit-speaking Indo-European tribes from the north, known as the Vedic people, who inhabited the Valley from roughly 1,800 BC to 1,000 BC. It is the Vedic age which really gives us our first firm links with anything specifically yogic. The concept of altering one's consciousness was a strong component of their world, and hymns dating from that time are full of references to practices which we would recognize as powerful meditations. The use of breath control, of quietening the normal thought processes by concentration and contemplation, of intense devotion; all are features of the activities of the Vedic seers. The hymns speak of overcoming the ego, abandoning the self, and being free to experience cosmic levels with the goal of complete enlightenment. In fact the origins of all the ideas which we think of as intrinsically 'yogic' are here. The Vedic hymns also contain specific ideas about the creation of the universe. The most important collections of hymns from the yogic point of view are the *Rig Veda* and the *Atharva-Veda*.

The people most concerned with these practices were the Vedic priests involved in ceremonial ritual and sacrifice. Also part of this society were less orthodox shaman figures, who were a throwback to more primitive times. By taking part in meditative practices, these shamans put themselves into ecstatic, trancelike states, which they associated with the spiritual world. Other groups on the religious fringes, which existed then, as now, would also have had their own forms of cult worship. One such group, a mysterious all-male brotherhood called the *Vratyas*, roamed the countryside rather like spiritual outlaws. They had a connection with yoga through their precise knowledge of breath control and its effect on mental and physical function.

KINGS AND BRAHMINS – MYSTICAL USERS OF TRANSCENDENTAL POWER

Vedic society used formal rituals in order to attain spiritual transformation. From about eight hundred BC, however, a rather more mystical trend came into being with the people responsible for some of yoga's most important literary works, the *Upanishads*. These people represented a kind of breakaway group, many of them from the ruling classes but some already living in isolation, and their concept of life and spirituality was fundamentally different to all that had gone before. They were seekers after a more internalized form of spiritual knowledge, perhaps more akin to self-realization as we know it today than to religious sanctity. While contemplation and meditation were still fundamental practices, these were used to bring about a connection with an indwelling, unchanging self at the centre of man's being, rather than with an external, universal one.

The *Upanishads* themselves comprise around two hundred mystical writings. The earliest of these were written in the eighth century BC; they have been added to throughout time, right up to the present century. Like similar texts, they simply note what had formally been a secret, oral tradition, very carefully guarded, passed on from inspired teacher to deserving disciple. Practical ways and means of achieving enlightenment were not a major feature of the first stages of this literature. Instead, they deal more with the nature of the universe, its deities – including its feminine aspect – and the concept of renunciation. They speak of the immortality of the soul, of transcendence of the mortal self, of separation from the finite world. They tell of divine revelation and the power of spiritual practice, of the sacrifice of mortal pleasure to ultimate bliss. It was the later texts that became much more specific regarding actual practice.

The *Upanishads* contain what is known as *Vedanta* philosophy; *Vedanta* meaning Veda's end – the conclusion of the Vedic world.

BUDDHISTS AND JAINS – PART OF THE YOGA FOLD

The movements and developments described so far were all embraced within the wide-ranging Hindu culture, which was beginning at this time to form its own religious identity. Buddhism and Jainism were also emerging. Although to a large extent rival religions, their emergence from the umbrella of Hinduism gave them a natural affinity with yogic thought. Jainism originated in the sixth century BC and is marked by extreme moral and ethical rules.

The idea of *karma* (which has become almost a cliché today) has always been central to the Jain religion. The aim of Jain spiritual practice is to go beyond a subservience to karmic activity – that is, to reach a state where one's actions do not cause repeated effects; that is, to go beyond being continually at the mercy of karmic activity. Strict adherence to ethical behaviour is the chief way of achieving this freedom. These ethical practices have been incorporated into yoga in the form of a system of disciplined restraints and observances (*See Chapter 5*). Jainism is a comparatively practical path, suitable for those who do not ultimately wish to renounce normal life, and thus it also fits current specifications for yoga practitioners. Nevertheless, it does emphasize self-control in the interests of achieving oneness with the 'Universal'.

Buddhism, which also arose in the sixth century BC, grew out of the teachings of Gautama the Buddha, an aristocrat born in northern India who could not accept orthodox Vedic tradition. In some Sanskrit literature Gautama is referred to as a 'yogin' – a practitioner of yoga.

The Buddha himself reached a state of enlightenment or *nirvana* – the transcendence of the self which is the goal of yoga. The Buddhist path is essentially a practical one which, a millennium and a half later, still makes sense to millions of people and has a growing following in the West. It consists of eight correct mental and physical practices, to be carried out simultaneously. Its moral guidelines and concentration techniques are very yogic in style, and Buddhism also teaches correct body posture for meditation.

EPICS AND ESOTERICA – THE FULL FORCE OF YOGIC THOUGHT

The national epics of India are called the *Ramayana* and the *Mahabharata*. These two lengthy tales contain the most essential yogic concepts and act as primary source books for yoga philosophy. Sections of these are also practical guides to specific yoga paths. The epics, rather like the plays of Shakespeare, are constantly being reinterpreted and performed, and there are many people who can recite them by heart. These epics are consistently popular; for example, Peter Brook's version of the *Mahabharata* has been performed over several hours in the British theatre and also transmitted on television.

The *Ramayana* was written by Valmiki, who was said to be a thief who was reformed by meditation, some time in the fifth or sixth century BC. Its hero is the figure of Rama, who embodies the qualities of moral purity, self-restraint and detachment from the world. A kind of archetypal ascetic, he is also a symbol for one of the three main Hindu deities: the preserver of the universe, Vishnu.

The *Mahabharata* also dates from the fifth century BC although it was not written down until roughly the second century AD. The *Mahabharata* tells the story of a war between two peoples, the Pandavas and the Kauravas, which was supposed to have occurred around one thousand BC. Prince Yudhishthira, one of the five Pandava sons, loses everything he has due to trickery and is banished from his kingdom, along with his brothers. After 13 years they return, seeking revenge and the restoration of their land from its usurper, King Dhrishtarashtra, and his powerful sons. After 18 days of fierce warfare they are successful. The story is read not just as a piece of thrilling history, but is interpreted symbolically as the essential struggle between good and evil.

The *Mahabharata* is also important for containing the *Bhagavad-Gita* ('The Lord's Song'), which may at one time have formed a separate story. The *Bhagavad-Gita* is one of the most important yoga texts. It takes the form of a conversation between the god Krishna, one of the incarnations of Vishnu, and one of the Pandava brothers, Prince Arjuna. A synthesis between spiritual goals and mundane activity is embodied within the dialogue, as Arjuna is instructed by Krishna in the correct ways to live fully and meaningfully in the world, while also encouraging 'non-attachment' to what he might gain from it. The essential theme is how to act in the world in full consciousness of the divine.

The *Mahabharata* also contains a section entitled *Moksha-Dharma* which relates to yoga theory. It speaks of basic things like a cleansing diet and breath control, deals with mental obstacles to the spiritual path, such as anger, doubt and fear, and warns against the possibility of being sidetracked into mistaking the development of psychic powers for true transformation. The *Moksha-Dharma* also includes instruction on how to concentrate and still the mind against external influences.

Meanwhile the Upanishadic literature continued to develop. In the fifth century BC, the important *Kathaka Upanishad* was written. The first truly yogic *Upanishad*, it deals specifically with the innermost self at the core of the human being, saying this 'self' forms the only true nature and that one should work consistently towards making everything else subservient to it.

Other *Upanishads* from this time are the *Shvetashvatara*, which deals with the process of meditation, the *Maitrayaniya*, which elucidates specific ways of uniting with the central 'self' through the use of energy channels, and the *Mandukya*, which is concerned with the chanting of the sacred 'om' sound.

PATANJALI'S PRACTICAL WISDOM.

Patanjali was probably a teacher of yoga, well versed in the subject both philosophically and experientially. His dates are speculative – some authorities put him 200 to 300 years before Christ, others say he wrote around 200 AD. Patanjali's *Yoga Sutras* are a compilation of yogic wisdom. Not necessarily original thoughts, they are a series of brief aphorisms condensing everything that had evolved about yoga up to that time.

The most important thing about Patanjali was that he gave yoga an organized framework. From his time onwards, yoga became a recognized 'system' rather than a series of amorphous philosophical and spiritual speculations which had been attached to other practices. Patanjali had a huge influence on the development of yoga and his system became known as

Classical Yoga. The philosophical side of yoga today is by and large Patanjali's system, with its precise concepts of the nature of the real self, the illusion of reality, and the possibility of transcendence. The *Yoga Sutras* is a short work: a brief 195 aphorisms in four chapters dealing with yoga's spiritual aim, its practice, the powers it brings forth, and how it can bring about freedom and transformation. The *sutras* (which can also be translated as 'threads') are designed to be concise aide-mémoires, rather than elaborations on the meaning and structure of the yoga system. Originally the aphorisms would have been learned by heart, and elucidated by the teacher.

Patanjali's *Yoga Sutras* have been the subject of extensive commentary throughout the ages. In fact it is essential to study them and add various explanations in order to unlock their meaning and know what to do in practice. Examples of Patanjali's succinct expression are: 'Yoga is the control of thought-waves in the mind', 'Wrong knowledge is knowledge which is false and not based upon the true nature of its object,' and 'Non-attachment is self-mastery; it is freedom from desire for what is seen or heard.'

In the *Yoga Sutras* we find the eight limbs of yoga which are still taught today by classical yoga instructors. These are restraints and disciplines (*yama* and *niyama*, or moral and ethical 'do's and don'ts' of life); posture (the *asanas* which most yoga classes concentrate on); breath control; the three steps to spiritual freedom: *pratyahara* (sense-withdrawal), *dharana* (concentration) and *dhyana* (meditation); and the ultimate goal, the bliss of liberation or the state of *samadhi*. All of these naturally integrate with each other and the practice of one tends to spill over into another. Gradually, if you practise yoga seriously enough, you will find yourself needing or even spontaneously experiencing something of each of these 'limbs', although the final stage of bliss is not guaranteed unless you are particularly dedicated!

Patanjali lived at a time of upheaval when many philosophies and systems were vying for popularity. His writings are the reason why yoga took its place as a serious part of the moral and spiritual map and why it has survived.

COUNTERING PATANJALI – THE YOGA UPANISHADS

Patanjali managed to extract the basic principles from the many varieties of yoga and construct out of these an essentially practical, simplified system. But his was not the only voice of yoga. His philosophical ideas were, in fact, quite contrary to mainstream Vedanta, as expressed previously in the *Upanishads*. Patanjali tended towards a dualistic viewpoint, where there is a struggle between two powers, those of the 'self' (the real being, that is, rather than the personality) and the forces of nature, from which we must seek to become liberated.

The *Upanishads*, however, uphold a world view in which everything is contained in an essential oneness. The *Yoga Upanishads*, which came after Patanjali, continue to centre on a kind of ecstatic realization, mainly based on harnessing the powers of sound and light. These also focus considerably on the energy system of the body, which can be used as a kind of power generator if one is aware of the correct techniques for breathing and profoundly tuning the mind.

These *Yoga Upanishads* are the forerunners of what came to be known as *kundalini* yoga. This is usually only practised by visionaries and adepts, but can be used in a diluted form for healing and restoring physical and mental capacities. Many of the later *Yoga Upanishads* deal specifically with methods of drawing up the 'life force' through the physical body until it reaches the top of the head and a blissful state of unity can be experienced. In a sense, then, the *Yoga Upanishads* have become very much part of mainstream yoga today (albeit tending towards the more esoteric variations); nowadays we are particularly interested in the power of the human body, and ways of harnessing and conducting that human power seem more accessible than dealing with the more abstract powers of the universe.

THE SPLITTING OF THE WAYS – FROM ABSTINENCE TO ORGIES

Yoga after Patanjali has a great variety of teachings and writings. One strong split that evolved was between what became known as the 'right-hand' and the 'left-hand' paths. While the right-hand path shunned, and some might say repressed, the existence of evil, the exponents of the left-hand path espoused it. For both, the goal of attaining oneness or spiritual unity was all-important, but how they did this was very different.

The left-handed way, in particular, embraced human sexuality and used it in ritual practices to achieve a state of ecstasy. Many sects in the beginning centuries of this millennium initiated bizarre practices to show how they could transcend the forbidden by direct experience of it. But along with these sects existed other traditions which employed more peaceful means of attaining bliss and spiritual harmony. Among these were the Shiva worshippers, whose practices led to the *siddha* yoga methods of contacting divine love which are now taught in the West.

Over the years up to the present time, yoga has really embraced a whole gamut of practices. There are stories of yoga practitioners who behaved like madmen, making obscene gestures and sounds and deliberately shocking the public. Others participated in ecstatic singing and dancing. Some ascetic sects lived far away from normal communities. Other groups would perform magic rituals with corpses and skulls, get ritually drunk, and take part in regular sexual orgies. Many advocated the sexual practice of retaining semen during sexual intercourse. Spiritual unity was perceived as being accessible through anything from sexual bliss to total isolation.

Some yogis sat in meditation on divine peace. At other times in history, yogic groups have agitated for social reforms, such as a change in the caste system and an end to inequality. Others were more intellectual, gaining their inspiration from reciting spiritual literature. Some shunned normal activities, others rejected all formal ritual. It was possible to be a yogi and believe in complex systems of practice, or to lead a life of simple devotion. Some became naked beggars, others led the life of a normal householder. But the ultimate goal of all these practices was transcendence and enlightenment.

TANTRA TODAY

The *tantric* path holds great appeal for the modern mind. *Tantra* is most commonly associated with fairly bizarre and liberal sexual debauchery, but that tends to be a popular exaggeration. In fact, the tantric philosophy which arose in the first century AD was simply concerned with embracing human bodily pleasures. It was originally predominantly a movement of the Indian working class, who had rejected the complicated philosophical ideas of the time and sought a more simple approach to spirituality.

Like the predominant Vedanta philosophy, and contrary to Patanjali, *tantra* was based on a non-dualist belief – that oneness exists as a universal power. It saw the life of the human form as embodying the divine, and while sexual practice was part of this, it was used only as one of many ways to raise the consciousness. The tantricists were the first to put forward specific models of the life force residing within the body, with its breath pathways, its subtle energy centres and the *kundalini* system which rises from the bottom of the spine to the crown of the head. *Tantra* also introduced methods of body purification and employed the use of sound, gesture (particular hand positions designed to balance and contain power), and pictorial designs which aimed to alter the energy system.

The sexual practices of *tantra* were indeed uninhibited and pleasurable. But they were also designed as complex rituals in which the lower self, with its fears, lusts and sensuality, was to be mastered. The partners partaking in the sexual act were encouraged to meditate on the divinity within themselves. They were trained to control and harmonize their subtle energy systems and to avoid the temporary pleasure of orgasm so that ultimate bliss could be attained.

Hatha yoga as practised today may not demand the rites of *tantra*, but it has much in common with its ideology. We are accustomed to using and celebrating the human body rather than trying to shun it, as the spiritual aspirants of the distant past were enjoined to do. Today, the idea of getting away from our bodies seems a strange concept. The Tantricists would have agreed with us. Their main task, one which appeals to us today, was to gain some measure of control so their bodies could work *for* them, rather than ruling them. Their idea was to utilize and amplify the subtle powers contained in the human system. The *hatha* yoga methods of becoming directly aware of the energy that lies within us, and strengthening and harmonizing it, are a direct development from medieval times when the Tantricists were in their prime.

THE RISE OF MODERN YOGA

As we have seen, *hatha* yoga is just a small part of yoga as a whole. However, this is the form we concentrate on today. While yoga's many streams of philosophy and ideology are distilled within *hatha* yoga, the practices controlling the body's energy system are those taught to most modern yoga practitioners.

Hatha yoga is said to have developed from a man called Goraksha, who lived in the tenth century AD. A legendary figure, he was known as a charismatic healer and a celibate. He is said to have written a work called *Hatha-Yoga* and various other works are attributed to him, however none of these are extant. We only know that from this time the specific practices of *hatha* yoga were set out. Interestingly, in his *Yoga Sutras* Patanjali glosses over the technicalities of practice.

The *Hatha Yoga Pradipika* is the best known work of classical yoga practice. Dating from the mid-fourteenth century AD, it describes the basic cleansing methods of the body, breath control methods, *mudras* or energy-controlling hand positions, and ways of holding specific areas of the body in order to intensify the life energy. It also goes through in detail the postures as we know them today.

Another classic text is called the *Gheranda-Samhita*, which was written in the seventeenth century. This lists various forms of physical purification, including that of the internal passages and organs. This text states that there are around 840,000 yoga postures, but that (perhaps thankfully) only 84 of these are important. The *Gheranda-Samhita* is at variance to Patanjali in stating that there are only seven, rather than eight limbs. The correct diet and environment are considered by its author, Sage Gheranda, to be very important for yoga practitioners, and he also gives clear instructions for very distinctive breath control practices. Correct use of the complete body is the focus of the *hatha* yoga that derives from these works, but, again, the ultimate goal is liberation.

YOGA IN THE WEST

Today, yoga seems to have been taken up enthusiastically by Westerners. The century that saw the colonization of India did much to bring 'foreign' ideas and practices to this country. The important Indian sage, Swami Vivekananda, travelled in the West in the 19th century and brought yogic ideas to a wide audience. Queen Victoria was very interested in yoga and would summon Indian sages to perform their strange body contortions.

Yoga really took off however after Swami Sivananda, one of the great Indian yoga practitioners, sent his disciple, Swami Vishnudevananda, to the West to spread yoga in the 1950s. The time was right. Universal spiritual ideas were becoming fashionable, along with interest in techniques of self-realization and the growth of health and body consciousness. Yoga was the ideal way to incorporate all these, and the 1960s and 1970s saw an enormous growth in the yoga 'industry'.

Other modern masters who have influenced the way yoga is taught in the west are BKS Iyengar, with his precise teaching of strongly-held yoga postures, and Desikachar who emphasizes pose and counter-pose along with controlled breathing. Pramahamsa Yogananda has also inspired many Westerners on the spiritual yogic path with his book, *Autobiography of a Yogi*. Other yoga practitioners have founded schools based around meditation rather than *hatha* yoga.

Gone are the days when doing yoga meant dedicating your life to weird and wonderful practices or isolating yourself from family and friends. Today, the most separation from normal life that comes about is often only an hour or so at an evening institute or health club yoga class, once a week. But this is not to denigrate modern yoga teaching. If the ancient wisdom of the East can reach the suburban High Streets of England, something is showing us that it must be needed and has a part to play. Relaxation, peace of mind, health and fitness may be the primary aims of the modern yoga student. But the age-old goals of taking charge of energy systems at play within us, and in the universe around us, are still there. Through consistent yoga practice we get our own taste of these in a way that fits our life and times.

3

YOGA IN PRACTICE
THE MANY PATHS OF YOGA

All forms of yoga have the same aim – a deep realization of the spiritual truths that lie behind existence. Practising yoga entails living more and more effectively in accordance with these truths. But just as there are all sorts of personalities and a whole variety of lifestyles, so there are different yogic paths to suit these.

Classically, four paths are described – *karma*, the yoga of work; *bhakti*, the yoga of devotion; *jnana*, the path of knowledge; and *raja*, the royal path. Different authorities add subdivisions and supplements. As specific ways of living these paths may seem irrelevant to modern life. The practices are intense and the dedication required to follow them rigidly would turn us into social outcasts. All the same, we can be aware of the fundamental ideas behind these paths, which in some form do filter through to our own lives. Rather than giving everything to one or another system, as did the practitioners of old, it is more useful for us to see that a modern synthesis of these is evolving – and to look at how we can manifest this synthesis for ourselves.

The ancient divisions between types of yoga hold true, but they are not rigid barriers. In fact there is a variety of views on how to use the yoga pathways. Some people interpret them as forming a stepladder, so that you move from system to system, mastering each in turn and evolving spiritually through increasing challenges. Others say they are to be used in conjunction with each other, and that the practitioner will develop the qualities which each system emphasizes simultaneously. Yet again, other authorities suggest that it is best to make a choice, or, preferably, to have the choice made for you by an enlightened master who can see which pathway is most suitable for you.

What kind of choices does the modern practitioner have? Our 'yoga' is predominantly *hatha*, the yoga of physical posture. But other kinds have infiltrated the West. If you are motivated you can find teachers of yogas which emphasize the use of sound and chanting, of love and devotion, of the mind rather than the body. In fact we gain a sense of the wholeness of yoga whatever system we follow. The full integration of yoga is something that is felt rather than taught. The various forms simply put their emphasis on different practices. It makes sense to use methods you enjoy and are in tune with. But the inner experiences of becoming more aware, wise, and in touch with yourself are universal.

KARMA YOGA – WORKING WITH A WILL

Karma Yoga is often described as the yoga of action. This is the way in which people leading ordinary lives, with jobs and families, can get their experience of yoga's ultimate truths. It is particularly suitable for Westerners as it combines the 'work ethic' with an underlying spirituality.

Over and above its 'hippie' connotations, the word *karma* denotes many important concepts. The common suggestion that it implies a willing acceptance of fate is really a distortion.

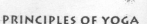

The word derives from the Sanskrit root *kri*, which means to make or to do, and it has a wide span of meanings. Essentially, *karma* yoga is about carrying out the actions of normal life while freeing yourself from the desire for personal gain.

To have a sense of *karma* yoga, it is important first of all to understand the idea of cause and effect that is embedded in *karma*. Actions cause results. This is easy to see in quite normal, everyday situations where our activities have caused pain or pleasure, or where a certain idea has borne fruit. As I sit down to write this book, for instance, I am aware that the mass of ideas in my head, which in turn came from my teachers and personal experience, will become words on a computer screen which will be turned into a book. You will then pick it up, be interested enough to spend money on it, take it home and be inspired, enthused and maybe even changed by some of the things it says. We can see quite clearly how everything in this world is in a state of constant evolution, and that to some extent we are in charge of how it evolves.

What is more difficult is to see how this works behind the scenes, in more esoteric realms. Here it helps to turn to psychology, which explains that what happens is often the result of inner processes of which we are unaware. The intentions we consciously express may often be quite contrary to what is going on inside us – yet deeply buried attitudes are usually betrayed by what we do, how we behave and even the words we use to express ourselves. Thus all these levels of our being, even down to our thought processes, are able to affect our lives and those of others. Looking again at this book, if I feel tired or bored with what I am writing, that will come across to the reader. You may find your own mind wandering. But if I am fired up by something I want to express, it will come across more strongly.

Taking a 'cosmic leap', we can look at these ever more subtle processes as having a kind of universal knock-on effect. There seems no doubt that we are far more powerful than we like to imagine. Our infinite abilities for creation and destruction are discernible in the physical world, from the making of bombs to babies. What is harder to conceptualize is how these abilities manifest themselves in the realms which we don't yet recognize, and this is precisely what *karma* yoga is interested in.

Given, then, that our world is like a continual game of consequences, the question is how do we play the game in the best possible way? Since the aim of yoga is liberation from states of 'unreality', and the attainment of a spiritual state of consciousness, the answer is that we remove ourselves from the 'game' altogether. In yoga terms, there is a state beyond this constant bumping of one action into another, where cause and effect cease. If we are always causing fresh effects, and some of these, because of our very nature as imperfect beings, are not exactly desirable, it follows that we try to create as little of a stir in the universe as possible.

But this is a tall order to start with. This is why *karma* yoga, in all its practicality, suggests that we use normal situations but treat them differently. Usually we work, for example, with our minds on the gains we are hoping for as a result – whether material, in the form of a large pay cheque, or personal – such as praise, recognition, fame. It is possible, with a little self-discipline, to catch yourself in these moments of being 'elsewhere' – that is, bored or not concentrating on the work in hand, but just thinking about the results. No one would suggest, in the modern world, that we work for inappropriate recompense; instead, the idea is to find a balance where you are not so focused on your own desires, so the work of *karma* yoga involves watching *how* you perform the activities of daily life, and especially becoming aware of the attitudes that lie beneath your actions. In this way, you gradually become more in touch with the kind of consequences your actions are creating.

We may realize in the course of this analysis that we are creating a few undesirable ripples for ourselves and others. We may also conclude that, in the end, even the pleasurable results which we think so important are just part of an interminable pattern of ups and downs. Do we want to continue to be part of that roller coaster, or do we want to experience something more stable, something yoga considers the 'real' reality?

Karma yoga proposes that if you remove yourself from goals that are purely personal, and ultimately detach yourself from any goal at all, it is possible to experience liberation from that endless round of cause and effect. Not only do we cease setting up more and more *karma*, or effects, to deal with in this life; we also prevent problems in subsequent incarnations. *Karma* yoga believes that practising this detachment from reward in your normal, everyday life leaves the way clear for ultimate transformation.

The principles of *karma* yoga are set out most succinctly in the *Bhagavad-Gita*, which is a section of the epic *Mahabharata*. Here the warrior Arjuna, who has to go to war, questions the god Krishna as to how to carry out this task in the most spiritual way. Krishna exhorts him to offer his duties in the dedicated sense of selfless action.

BHAKTI YOGA – THE LOVING ECSTATIC

Once you have mastered the art of doing your practical work in the right spirit, advocates of the stepladder path say you are ready for *bhakti* yoga. While *karma* yoga has a strengthening effect, *bhakti* is the path of pure devotion. Sometimes it is advised only for people who have an emotional, sensitive nature, who would rather act from the heart rather than the head; non-intellectuals who are easily attracted to the power of ecstatic prayer.

Culturally, *bhakti* yoga is a far cry from Western European life. But although its origins are in the ancient religious practices of South India, in essence it has elements which link it with our present psychology. *Bhakti* may well be the oldest form of yoga, but we can still relate to the importance of emotional expression. What we do not do so well today is use our passions and feelings so that they have a positive outcome and help our spiritual growth.

Bhakti grew up amongst the ordinary people, who reacted against formalized Vedic priestly ritual. These people responded to more personal gods, in particular Vishnu and Shiva, who were represented as real (albeit mythological) figures and therefore were regarded as 'tangible' aspects of the divinity. The most important aspect of their worship was an intense, devotional state of mind, where they would concentrate on the deity and attempt to merge with it, thus reaching way beyond individual consciousness. This use of emotional expression, including all the drama and passion of love, was thoroughly permissible as long as it was ultimately directed in a self-transcending way towards the spiritual dimension. Rather than shutting out the world of human feeling, *bhakti* yogis used it as a means of reaching a higher ideal.

It is the simplicity of using this outflow of human emotion that makes us sympathetic to the *bhakti* way. But although woven into the fabric of Indian religion and tradition, it has also developed as a very subtle system in its own right. It grew up classically into a formalized set of stages each one of which needs extreme concentration to be put into effect correctly. As delineated in the ninth century AD, these include chanting songs of praise, ritual ceremonies, prostration and expressions of longing, closeness and intimacy with the divine.

Practitioners of *bhakti* yoga are, to begin with, permitted some degree of personal motivation. Deep longing is, after all, usually initiated by personal desire. Gradually however, the aspirant becomes free of any selfishness and more and more enveloped in an all-pervading love which goes far beyond the self. The *bhakti* path has much in common with other mystical movements where the focus is heartfelt devotion, such as the Sufi and the Hasidic. Like these it was never part of the mainstream religious life. The Biblical *Song of Songs*, with its longing for the divine set in the form of a love poem, can be seen, amongst other interpretations, as a great example of *bhakti* expression.

JNANA YOGA – KNOWING THE TRUTH

'Who am I?' is one of the great conundrums often meditated upon as a means of spiritual enlightenment. Through hours, weeks and even years of concentrated enquiry, you may come to an (often sudden) awareness of the originating universal force field behind the question. The 'Who am I' method, typically used in Zen, is one way of approaching *jnana* yoga, which is also termed the yoga of knowledge. The knowledge implied, however, is actually a knowing that is far deeper than intellectual learning. It is a felt understanding, a realization beyond belief systems, a transformational wisdom.

This does not mean that the intellect is dormant in the process. *Jnana* yoga is a recommended path for those of an enquiring mind, and powerfully driven, strong-willed people are traditionally most drawn to it. Pride, overambition and impulsiveness are said to be drawbacks to spiritual progress in these types of people, so they are enjoined to make determined efforts to overcome these personality traits.

The path of *jnana* yoga comes straight from the classical mainstream Indian Vedanta tradition. Its aim is complete identification with the divine. This divinity is not something outside yourself, as it is in *bhakti* yoga where it is the object of love and worship. The divine in *jnana* yoga is the inner mystery of all creation, the intelligent life force which lies behind all our illusions.

This divinity is reached by using the full force of the mind, turned inwards and enquiring into itself. It is said to be a difficult path; intense contemplation and meditation are fundamental requisites. Medieval texts say that the people who practise *jnana* yoga need to develop tranquillity and restraint, strong physical and mental endurance, a firmly focused mind and deep faith. It is primarily a mental art, achieving insight through the use of reason. Clarity, discernment and discrimination are the goals, along with a state in which ultimate reality can be distinguished from everything that is 'unreal'.

Although traditionally requiring long hours of focused contemplation, *jnana* yoga can be a powerful tool for this modern day and age. The desire for knowledge, the strong intellectual drive and workaholic tendencies which many people have, would make them ideal candidates for the intense spiritual enquiry of *jnana* yoga; for taking steps beyond the amassing of information, and applying the mind to what lies behind it. Seek out the essential truth which lies at the root of everything you think you know, and you have the basis of *jnana* yoga.

RAJA YOGA – KING OF THEM ALL

Raja is a rather late term in the history of yoga. It was the name given to the whole of Patanjali's system after he had evolved it, primarily describing how to quieten and concentrate the mind in order to uncover transcendental peace. *Raja* yoga is also sometimes used as a general term for meditation. Thus it is seen as separate from the physical postures of *hatha* yoga. Other sources however say that the physical area of yoga is an integral part of *raja* yoga.

With or without physical movement, *raja* yoga is said to be the 'royal path'. It is demanding. It is concerned with alerting you to the intricate shifts of the mental processes, and showing how to gain mastery over them. Some authorities insist that anyone who goes in for the rigours of this kind of discipline should already have attained the ability to control the body, actions and emotions through *hatha, karma* and *bhạkti* yoga. Others teach that *hatha* and *raja* yoga are foundation stones, and that these body/mind disciplines should lead the way to more esoteric practices.

Raja yoga delves deeply into the recesses of the mind. It appeals to the modern consciousness because of our interest in mental processes. But it has a different focus to that of the psychotherapies. Rather than examining and 'working through' various states of mind, *raja* yoga seeks alignment with an overriding state of stability, beyond the disturbances of emotions.

Step one of this process is being able to recognize the false layers, often referred to as veils, which obscure the true self. In psychological terms these might be seen as identifying with one's emotions. We may describe ourselves as 'angry', 'frightened', 'nervous', 'temperamental', and so on. Often we attribute our state to all sorts of origins whether through heredity, habit, or just basic personality. In the light of *raja* yoga, however, we can see we are simply experiencing the effects of these states as a disturbance to our profoundly peaceful selves. *Raja* yoga does not deny these traits their reality, but sees them as temporary ripples on a placid lake. It aims to become very aware of them as they arise, and gradually to effect a process of dismantling and dissolution of these disturbances. Perception, will and intuition are all employed in this path.

Patanjali called his own teaching *astanga* yoga – the eight-limbed path. His specific disciplines include simple ethical rules such as honesty, nonviolence and cleanliness. Then follows the practice of comfortable physical posture ('a firm seat'), control of the breath, and deactivating the senses so they do not impinge on the mind's tranquillity. The last three stages of Patanjali's 'royal' path to supra-consciousness are the hardest. They form a structured development starting with concentration, where the mind focuses without distraction, contemplation where you reach an intensely absorbed state, and meditation which arrives as a consequence of the others, where you are 'at one', with no sense of separation from anything.

This final stage, known in Sanskrit as *samadhi*, can be defined as ecstasy or bliss. It is the union that yoga is really all about. People who have experienced this state use descriptions like expansion, disappearance of the self, delight, super-wakefulness. Practices leading to *samadhi* were employed for many centuries prior to Patanjali's systemization, so we can be sure that in his work he covered the main ground of what had been hitherto somewhat separate approaches.

Nowadays meditation, and preparation for meditation, is our closest approach to the *raja* yoga path. For many people this path has been a lifeline, allowing them to see the mental disturbances of daily life for what they are – self-imposed barriers and stresses. While perhaps not reaching the extremes of ultimate bliss, those who meditate regularly are able to still the waves of the mind and reach a deep level of equanimity.

HATHA YOGA – PERFECTION THROUGH THE BODY

Hatha yoga controls and purifies the processes of the physical body in order to transform their powerful energies. It was referred to by Patanjali as part of his eight-limbed *raja* path, although only in passing. Patanjali gave no details about the complex postures which we know today as *hatha* yoga. It was left to the medieval writers to expound on these. Whether such later descriptions were what Patanjali was referring to or not is open to debate; suffice to say that all our detailed knowledge of *hatha* yoga practice comes from the later texts, the *Hatha Yoga Pradipika*, *Gheranda Samhita* and the *Siva Samhita*. They all say that *hatha* Yoga is a preparation for *raja* yoga. Most authorities agree that whether they are viewed as concurrent or separate practices, one should not be done without the other. At some stage *hatha* yoga was downgraded and given an inferior status; not seen as a real spiritual path. It became linked with magic and the abuse of power, and its *tantric* associations meant it was often viewed as decadent.

Nowadays we have come full circle. *Hatha* yoga's very accessibility has enhanced its popularity and because it is a less overtly 'spiritual' path it has become favoured. But it is a mistake to see *hatha* yoga as just body-oriented. It is *tantric* in that it uses the physical world rather than insisting on paths of rejection and withdrawal. But *tantra* doesn't stop there. A beautiful, energetic body may be gained in the process of *hatha* yoga, but should not be a goal in its own right. A strong mind and a released spirit in this healthy body are the spiritual aims.

Hatha yoga is said in the ancient texts to appeal to eager, enthusiastic people who are independent and sympathetic, understanding, courageous and honest. If you already possess these virtues, six years of practice should give you the means to spiritual liberation.

Hatha yoga consists of the well-known body postures, practised in a sequence which will differ according to whose authority you take. Generally, standing postures are performed first, then sitting postures, with relaxation at the end. Designed to give you the firm, unwavering posture necessary for meditation, they also affect the body's total energy flow. But there is more to *hatha* than physical twists and turns. Internal cleansing practices are also recommended as a first stage of purification. Modified forms of these can be practical today (*see Chapter 7, Yoga for Strength of Body*). Breathing practices (called *pranayama* in Sanskrit) are essential; these can be done both independently and while performing the postures. Breathing practices help the cleansing process, and much more besides. Breath is said to contain essential life force and how we take it in and use it is of supreme importance. All *hatha* yoga is ultimately designed to harness and control energy flow, whether by breathing, moving, or sitting still.

Also important in the practice are *bandhas*, or 'locks' which are applied to various areas of the body while the postures are held. These are muscle contractions, and they do exactly what they say – they lock energy into the system. The concentrated energy enhances the power of the posture. *Hatha* yoga is based on the fact that the body is a potent force. The energies which flow through the body range from those we can feel and tangibly express – such as the obvious physical and emotional energies – to the most subtle, of which we are unaware, but which help govern us nevertheless.

In *hatha* yoga we attempt to become aware of these energies, just as we seek to become aware of the mind waves in *raja* yoga. Once we have mastered this awareness we can begin to take charge of how we use these energies. It is rather as if the body were a power generator, with the energetic charges produced being refined and channelled as essential electricity supply. Only in this case, our own electricity system is being tuned in the high voltage direction of a change in consciousness. The subtle electrics of the body are called, in Sanskrit, *kundalini*. With careful control (and sometimes spontaneously) this force rises through the *chakra* system – the concentrated energy centres – until it culminates at the top of the head. With the subtle energies thus flowing freely, transcendence on the same lines as that brought about by other yogas can occur.

So *hatha* yoga works simultaneously on all the body systems. Musculature and bones, blood, respiration and nerves, subtle energy pathways that we are usually unaware of – all are involved. Ideally, these become so strong that they work without us having to worry about them, without tying us down in the physical world. They become ready conductors of finer energies, until eventually they are powerful enough to take more transformative forces. As you do the practices, you will certainly get some sense of what this feels like. Years of tension begin to shift, muscles soften and release. The spine lifts and lengthens, there is a spring in your step. You may feel slight tingling, vibrations or 'pins and needles'. This is a sign that energy is starting to move instead of being stuck, inert. And even if it is just renewed freedom to move the tangibly physical, the rewards of *hatha* yoga are immediate. *Hatha* is hard work but it is a familiar discipline: that of moving your body. It works slowly but surely. The more you do it, the more powerful you will become.

There are a number of other types of yoga, some of them offshoots of the main categories described above and others loosely overlapping them. *Kundalini* for instance is often associated with *hatha* yoga. The main distinctions lay in the kind of practices these yogas entail; the goals are all similar.

KUNDALINI – THE EXPLODING CONSCIOUSNESS

Kundalini yoga is sometimes spoken of as a separate entity. It refers to the specific practice of raising the *kundalini* force, the strong transformative energy which is believed to originate at the base of the spine and which uses the spinal cord as its conductor. *Kundalini* practitioners learn to control this force, to make it rise through each of the seven energy centres which between them govern the body's functions on all levels. When the energy is flowing naturally and well around all these centres, we experience health, balance and tremendous vitality.

The root *chakra*, at the perineum, is where the *kundalini* force originates. This controls the lower limbs and the sense of smell, as well as the emotion of fear and the sense of security. At the genitals, the base *chakra* governs sexuality and physical energy, the hands and the sense of taste. The navel *chakra* presides over vision, power and expansiveness. At the heart, the dominant force works on the sense of touch, compassion and love. The throat *chakra* energy controls the mouth and skin, the auditory sense and communication. It is connected to positive and negative attitudes to life. The 'third eye' *chakra* governs sensory input to the mind as well as our ability to trust. It is also the seat of wisdom and the connecting point between our selves and universal consciousness. The topmost centre, the crown *chakra*, is said to be all-transcending. From here, we are said to have the ability to transcend all 'separation'.

The psycho-spiritual *kundalini* force can be explosive. In

uncontrolled form, it can do anything from giving you blinding headaches to driving you insane. Although this sounds like a dramatic phenomenon, the *kundalini* experience is not unusual. Taking drugs can be a powerful way of unleashing it. It may also occur at times of great stress or crisis. Sensations of strong heat or pressure along the spinal column, visions and voices, while they may be alarming, do not necessarily herald physical and mental breakdown. Mystics, saints, geniuses and healers throughout the centuries have experienced these as physical manifestations of spiritual phenomena. But the *kundalini* can also unfold gently and safely, through proper meditation on the chakra centres.

TANTRA YOGA – AN ALL-EMBRACING POWER

Tantra yoga comes from the non-separatist school of thought which says we do not have to isolate ourselves in order to attain a degree of self-mastery. *Tantra* is not the path for those who shun the things of the world, the extreme ascetics and hermits. It belongs to the solid, basic world of the senses where the energy of the body and material things can connect with the spiritual.

Tantra uses all the power of our natural senses and desires, with the aim of transforming and harmonizing them. This, however, can only happen if we live out these desires fully without trying to circumvent or repress them. Not surprisingly, *tantra* fits well into the modern world and is probably the only form of yoga which most of us can honestly be said to practice. It covers in particular *hatha* and *raja* yoga.

Tantra yoga has also become somewhat synonymous with sexual yoga. Sexual intercourse is one of the most fundamental ways in which to use and transform energy. For many people the kind of transformative experiences that we talk about as 'spiritual' – devotion, unity, ecstasy – are most directly attainable through sex. It follows, then, that if we use the sexual experience with conscious awareness of the energy being unleashed, it can be one of the fastest routes to spiritual harmony. Ways of building power *tantrically* include experiencing the flow of energies between partners, directing them through the body rather than focusing on predominantly 'sexual' areas and concentrating on the moment instead of racing towards the goal of orgasm. Sexual *tantra* is therefore a way of increasing, containing and using one of the most accessible vital energies.

MANTRA YOGA – VIBRATING TO A DIFFERENT TUNE

Mantra yoga uses sound to create changes in consciousness. Creation itself is said to have begun with sound, which can be interpreted in its purest form as vibration. The sacred word OM is the most powerful sound of all. It employs all the areas of speech – the throat, mouth and lips – and every vocal sound. There are many levels to the OM chant, which is said to be capable of affecting body, soul and spirit.

Mantras are powerful sounds, like the OM chant, although these are specifically designed both for individual needs and for affecting various areas of the psyche. *Mantra* yoga was originally rather denigrated as being only suitable for 'men of small enterprise' – critical and timid types who were unable to do much else in terms of spiritual practice. The comparatively simple activity of repeating a sound is certainly less demanding than many other forms of yoga. It is, however, also extremely esoteric, and practitioners are warned that intention is all.

Parrot-fashion chants are unlikely to have the desired effect.

Sounds do not necessarily have to be chanted. They can be repeated silently and internally, said aloud or murmured to oneself. Silent and mindful repetition is supposed to be the best way. A *mantra* can be a word or several words. The Transcendental Meditation system (TM) is a powerful form of *mantra* yoga. Each sound is given personally, in accordance with the overall needs of the practitioner. It vibrates with a particular frequency which 'tunes' the recipient's energy system, making him more spiritually awake.

YANTRA YOGA – THE ART OF LOOKING DEEPLY

A *yantra* is a geometric design. Several of these designs joined together into an intricate pattern are called a *mandala*. Gazing with deep concentration on one of these can cause alterations in your state of consciousness. Each shape and colour, like the vibrations of sound, affects the different *chakras* or energies of the body.

The simple act of looking with awareness for a period of time on one of these designs will also help concentration, and lead to a meditative state. The looking should be done in a way that continually brings the mind back to the *mandala*, using it as a tool for keeping awake and aware and present. With practice, it is possible to experience a sense of blending and non-separateness.

LAYA YOGA – THE MERGED CONSCIOUSNESS

Laya yoga is a kind of intense, meditative state induced by abstinence, sense withdrawal and concentration. It has similarities to *tantra, hatha* and *raja* yoga. The experience is of mind dissolution: forgetting all previous impressions, ideas and separate identity, and becoming at one with a transcendental consciousness. *Laya* yoga was traditionally recommended for liberal-minded non-extremists. Although it works with the *kundalini* system of *chakras,* it is a gentle system of gradual transcendence.

SYNTHESIZED YOGA – THE MODERN VERSIONS

You are more likely nowadays to hear yoga systems referred to as Iyengar, Sivanada, Astanga Vinyasa and others. These names refer to the teachers who originated them, or to specific practices contained within them. They have taken the main elements from the classical tradition, emphasizing those which are relevant to our time and needs.

The Iyengar system is very popular. BKS Iyengar is an Indian teacher who has influenced many Westerners. His system is a synthesis of *hatha* and *raja,* which he feels are inter-dependent. Iyengar yoga is quite physically demanding, with great precision required for the performance of posture. Once mastered, it offers a complete means of tuning body, mind and spirit.

Sivanada Yoga, devised by Swami Vishnu Devananda from the teachings of his master, Swami Sivananda, is a set system of smooth-running breathing practices and postures. Diet and positive thinking are also emphasized.

Kripalu yoga is part of a holistic system of health from the work of Amrit Desai. It is a soft, flowing method emphasizing self-awareness, flexibility and relaxation.

Astanga Vinyasa is also known as 'power yoga'. It is suitable for the very fit, who want their yoga to act as a strong physical work-out, whilst also giving them the benefits of fluidity of movement and breath control. It claims to be the original *astanga* method meant by Patanjali and to encompass all the eight limbs, as outlined earlier. The postures are performed fast and continuously, with link movements, encouraging the build up of heat in the body and a strong flow of energy. This also means you have to concentrate so intensively that you experience a state of oneness.

Yoga for Health is based on the work of Howard Kent, of the Ickwell Bury foundation. It is an applied use of yoga for overall fitness of body and mind, and can be done by the disabled and those who are not used to rigorous physical disciplines. Mental attitudes and positive thinking are emphasized.

The British Wheel of Yoga system has become the official training method for yoga teachers in England. It concentrates on the correct performance of posture, in line with current safe health and fitness techniques. Teachers also have to be well versed in the classical practice and philosophy of yoga.

4

YOGA TO FREE THE SPIRIT

YOGA'S SPIRITUAL PHILOSOPHY

For the average Westerner living in a secular society, 'spirit' is a hazy concept. The spiritual side of life is often seen as going hand in hand with religious ritual. Although it can be a vital source of satisfaction and meaning, religious belief is on the decline and 'public' religious observance is becoming a minority interest. For most non-religious people, their spiritual life, if it exists at all, is a private matter.

When pressed, however, the majority of us would admit that we have some notion of what spirituality means. However this notion has evolved – whether we have been influenced by traditional religious ideas, or by our own experiences, perhaps mixed up with stories of the exorcism of ghosts, or contacting long-dead Aunt Mary – it is likely to be a highly personal view. Forming an individual connection with a creative force; raising yourself to higher aspects of your own nature; finding peace; these are just a few contemporary interpretations of spirituality.

The swing that many have made away from organized religion towards defining a more personal spiritual meaning has encouraged those interested in the spiritual life to find out more about mystical movements. The mystical search has always been a predominantly personal one. Traditionally the individual seeker on the path would go through a variety of transformative experiences, leading to direct association (or even unity) with a transcendental force. It is this direct, personal experience which we seem to crave today.

This desire for direct spiritual experience has led many people to look to the religious systems of the East. These seem to lend themselves more easily to personal realization than do the social and communal demands of organized Western religion. The personal mystical experience has always had more credence in mainstream Eastern thought, while anything deemed esoteric has been kept under secretive wraps in Western traditions.

'New Age' thinking has taken on board many ideas about self-transformation from different cultures, especially Eastern ones. It has almost become a new religion. The way it has synthesized and reformulated many hitherto esoteric traditions means they have now become public knowledge. Adherents of Buddhism, chanting, Sufi dancing and the like can be found in towns and cities across the world. Yoga is very much part of this world.

The New Age ethos is largely concerned with ridding the self of the restrictions of conditioning and finding oneself – however one might define that 'self'. A more universal application of this ethos carries the ideals of world harmony, peace and unity. All these concepts are redefinitions of ideas rooted in religious understanding. Yoga's strong role in both the contemporary New Age scene and in fundamental Hindu philosophy shows that there is nothing new in the Universe. Our need to contact something higher or more permanent than ourselves, and to find some expression for that connection, lives in the human psyche now as it did three thousand years ago.

DEVELOPED BEINGS OF OLD – SUPERPOWERED SEERS

Amongst the Vedic peoples were *rishis* – visionaries, or seers with supra-normal powers. Like the prophets of the Bible, the *rishis* embody some of the oldest examples of the human desire and ability to live in other states of consciousness. The Vedic rites which developed reflected the universal order as these visionaries understood it; their purpose was to make it accessible to the people and impart its cosmic laws.

The Vedic system gradually became more elaborate and ceremonial. Genuine mystical experience eventually became less important than the intricacies of observance. The yoga that grew out of this became organized more formally, but kept at its heart the importance of contacting the spiritual dimension. Religious and philosophical ideas accordingly became more sophisticated and their different schools and practices merged as a system of which yoga was an integral part. At the root of this system was the wisdom of the Vedic masters, which gave rise to the Hindu religion.

RELIGION AND PHILOSOPHY – INDISPENSABLE PARTS OF THE YOGA TRADITION

Yoga is intimately bound up with Indian philosophy, which is a system of highly complex ideas, and so much part of India's multifaceted religious tradition that the two are inseparable. Within the Indian tradition, philosophy presents an active model of how the universe is structured. It speaks of the fundamental role of mankind, and how best one can play a part in this structure.

Thus Indian philosophy is more a blueprint for living than a set of theoretical ideas. The edges between yoga, philosophy and religion are blurred and often indistinguishable. While all great teachers insist that yoga is not a religion, it is part of a way of life that can be slanted towards the religious.

There are six main branches of Indian philosophy. These arose around 600–500BC, a time of universal cultural ferment coinciding with the rise of Greek and Hebrew civilizations. These Indian philosophical systems continued to develop and redefine themselves for hundreds of years. They all coexist and can be regarded as different standpoints from which to view the same reality. Yoga is one of these branches, or standpoints, and it represents the mystical tradition. It emphasizes a union between the personal, individual being and the universal consciousness.

Of the other philosophical schools, *Samkhya* is closest to yoga. Until the time of Patanjali, *Samkhya* was coupled with yoga. Their ideas are similar but they use different methodology. *Samkhya* is a more intellectual path, encouraging the process of accurate discrimination in order to reach the goal of discovering 'reality'. Yoga is more directed towards dynamic meditative processes. Where these schools converge is in their insistence that there are two major forces in the universe – the transcendental and the material. Within the material world there are also several subdivisions; all are linked by an interplay of vital qualities – active, passive and intelligent – called *gunas*. This idea contradicts the orthodox Vedic tradition, which holds to a distinctly non-dualistic world view.

The *Vedanta* (literally 'Veda's end') mode of philosophy, by contrast, says that 'all is everything' – we do not have to get beyond one state in order to realize another. Instead, we have to recognize that there is no separation. The method used to achieve this realization, or recognition, involves ritual practice.

In fact the Hindu philosophical schools are so tolerant of each other that Vedanta is often taught as part of yoga, with the emphasis shifting away from the traditional dualistic world view, towards the concept of an essential oneness. The leading light of Vedanta was the philosopher Shankara, who lived in the eighth century AD.

Other schools of philosophy are the *Mimamsa,* which focuses on morals and ethics as the guiding principles of the universe; the *Vaisheshika,* which teaches that we can gain liberation by understanding the specific distinctions between principles such as time and space; and *Nyaya,* a school of obtaining insight through logic and thought.

Yoga, then, is the mystical religious philosophy of India. How has it come to be so relevant to us today? It is difficult to know whether what we interpret as yogic ideas today would have been understood as such by the ancient sages of the Hindu culture. But although our relationship to these ideas may not be historically accurate, we have enough material to provide inspiring explanations which can help us make sense of our world. We have profound insights into universal spiritual knowledge, and guidelines for a lifetime of exploration.

'FAKING IT' – SPIRITUAL ESCAPISM

Yoga philosophy does not just map out the cosmos with our own known universe within it; it also deals with the inner world. Human consciousness, it maintains, is a reflection of the rest of reality. Deciphering yoga philosophy can therefore act as spiritual, as well as psychological growth. But here a word of warning is necessary. Spiritual exploration is not for people who are psychologically unsound. The search for spiritual truths can be a way of evading fundamental self-knowledge.

Any imbalances at personality level should be ironed out first.

True, a spiritual journey can activate the ability to do this. But if you leap into it too deeply and too soon, it can lead to an avoidance of personal problems. For instance, someone who has trouble relating to other people may find themselves using their 'spiritual' pursuit as an excuse to withdraw from the normal world. So turning to cosmic truths can have the negative effects of helping you mask your own truth, suppress emotional conflicts and compound inner confusions under a surface air of spiritual understanding. Before doing anything 'spiritual', take an honest look at yourself, your life and your relationships, and do some therapeutic work if necessary.

YOGA'S COSMIC ORDER

The Yogic master plan of the cosmos is a hierarchical system with several overlapping components.

PURUSHA (OR PURUSA)

Purusha is often referred to as 'Self', but it's a far cry from the self (with a small 's') of the personality, with all the traits which make us an individual. *Purusha* is 'Self' with a capital S, an unlimited state of being which belongs to the whole universe. It can be described many ways – the transcendental, pure consciousness, the numinous, the soul, spirit, infinite energy, awareness, the source, the Absolute. It is this which the yogic practitioner is trying to 'realize', to transform himself into, in the true sense of self-realization.

In some of the systems referred to previously, this Self is seen as being rather distant from the world of ordinary matter as we know it. Patanjali himself had problems with this because it is not easy to explain how to bridge the gap between these two states. However, both the greater Self and the world of matter are seen as having an eternal component: an intelligence which acts as a connecting force.

In many other yogic writings, however, the Self is very much a part of the whole being of the human and his sensory experiences. These schools of thought are more concerned with breaking the boundaries of self-limitation, in order to recognize what is both within and without. In later traditions, *purusha* became associated with the universal male principle; a more individuated consciousness concerned with activity.

Purusha can be seen as the original stuff of the universe, a pure energy which existed pre-creation. Everything else is a diminution of this, at the mercy of constant change and therefore subject to disharmony. The possibility of contacting this pivotal, central state of purity is at the heart of yoga's spiritual philosophy.

ATMAN

Some schools of thought split the Self up into several Selves. These are known as *atman*, which has a more tangible, individual connotation than *purusha*. These Selves have more in common with the human consciousness and are said to be directly responsible for it.

Atman has also been described as the psychic consciousness in man, which again makes it more accessible. However, in some systems *atman* is virtually synonymous with *purusha*. Through contacting *atman* in ourselves we are able to connect with the overriding principle of *purusha* to which it belongs.

BRAHMAN

Brahman is analogous to *atman*, but a slightly different concept. *Brahman* is the cosmic or divine principle, a vast super-conscious reality. Again, this idea is very similar to *purusha*, although the sense of *Brahman* is more that of a fundamental 'Absolute Being', in some ways similar to the concept of God. This 'Absolute' encompasses and acts as the guiding principle to all things.

However, *Brahman* is nothing like an overseeing father figure. It has a quality of immanence, of being present in the world while not of the world, rather than being fully transcendent or distant. Like *atman*, then, this concept is easier to grasp than the ineffability of *purusha*. We can relate to the Absolute as existing in our own being as well as 'out there'.

ISHVARA

Ishvara, according to Hindu philosophy, is strictly speaking a diluted form of *Brahman*. It can create, look after its creation, and destroy. It is most closely aligned to the Western idea of God and the word roughly means 'Lord'. Like God, it is important for providing a means to devotion.

Ishvara is also described as being one of a number of aspects of the infinite. Patanjali saw *ishvara* as being a special kind of *purusha*, singular in its awareness of being unaffected by ordinary forces.

PRAKRITI

Prakriti represents the structure of the world as we know it. You can look at *prakriti* as nature, matter, creation, existence, manifestation. It has also been seen as the feminine principle which developed into *tantric* thought. Even though it has more to do with the immediate world, *prakriti* is as eternal and indestructible as its counterpart, *purusha*. How is this so? At its core it has the same unchanging purity; but it has an additional facility – the ability to give rise to mutations.

This idea of mutation is fundamental to the Hindu system of death and rebirth. As live beings we are in the creative phase of *prakriti*. When we die, we return to its eternal form. The trick is to be able to live in consciousness of what is eternal, even though in order to exist at all we have to be in a fundamentally transitory state. As part of nature, we are cut off from the direct source but ultimately we belong to it. To use the elephant analogy from the beginning of Chapter One, we can exist as tail, ears or skin, yet we must seek to be aware that we are the whole animal.

The difference – or the unity – between *prakriti* and *purusha* forms the basis of the dualistic or non-dualistic approaches of Indian philosophy. According to classical yoga, we have to evolve through *prakriti*'s world of matter in order to reach the world of Self.

THE GUNAS

The *gunas* are the three forces inherent in *prakriti*. They have variously been described as attributes, qualities, properties, energies, strands, building blocks, entities, atoms, material, causal urges – take your pick. When *prakriti* is in its unchanging form, the *gunas* exist in perfect balance with each other. When *prakriti* becomes creative, they interact and one or the other will predominate.

However you define the *gunas*, they are readily discernible in the real world. The guna of *rajas* is active, passionate, restless and stimulating. The *tamas* guna is passive, withdrawn, solid and resistant. *Sattva* is the guna of basic intelligence. It is, if you like, the central axis of the *guna* 'seesaw', providing balance, order, control and peace. It represents purity and light. A *sattvic* predominance, therefore, is the one to aim for.

The *gunas* are in a constantly changing relationship. They come into play in everything you can name, from human behaviour and feelings to music, colours, plants and food. You can experiment with trying to notice how these qualities manifest themselves in everyday life. Children for instance are inherently *rajasic*, but they can also become *tamasic* if ill, troubled or out of sorts. We ourselves can easily swing from one to the other during the course of a day.

We can start to develop spiritual awareness by taking careful note of how we are at any one time; not in a judgmental way but simply in a spirit of objectivity. Doing this in a state of peaceful observation will in itself enhance your ability to come back into a state of *sattvic* centredness. The quality of *sattva* is the one which is said to link *prakriti* with *purusha*, and so the more you manifest it in your life the more access you will have to the 'Transcendent Self'.

TOWARDS PERSONAL ORDER – YOGA'S GRAND PLAN OF THE PSYCHE

As well as providing a map of cosmic reality, yoga says much about the nature of the personal self, known in Sanskrit as *jiva*. In one way we can see our 'self', with its individual psychology, as a mirror of the cosmic order. Just as the cosmos has elements that are both eternal and unchanging, as well as creative and changing, so we also embody these principles. At its highest level the soul, or the Higher Self, continues even when the body becomes 'dust to dust'. This is a fundamental belief in all spiritual systems. At other levels we can see how our children, or our works, or our ideas, live on after us, and many of us feel these to be our true link with eternity.

While yoga does not claim to be a psychology in its own right, it can offer an alternative system for explaining the way we are. Conditioning, emotions, unconscious drives – all have their parallels in the yogic scheme of things, and so do methods of dealing with them.

THE MIND

Yoga psychology divides the mind into four areas. *Manas* is the lower mind; the place of conscious, everyday thoughts. *Manas* links our perceptions and actions with the second area, *buddhi*, which enables us to use intellectual discrimination. *Buddhi* is also a cosmic or higher intelligence which can remind us of the wisdom, or otherwise, of our actions. After this comes *ahamkara*, the ego, which has individual, 'I'-centred thoughts and preferences. *Citta*, the fourth area, is where all the stuff of the mind is received and stored. It is the closest that the yoga model comes to the idea of the unconscious. Our conditioning comes from the realm of *citta*.

VRITTIS

Vrittis are the thought waves of the mind. Patanjali was concerned specifically with the *vrittis*, likening them to disturbing ripples across what would be naturally calm waters. The *Yoga Sutras* deal at length with ways of eliminating these waves so that we can return to a clear, equable state. According to Patanjali, the work of achieving a steady, undisturbed mind was one of the most important paths to liberation.

SAMSKARAS

In yoga, the unconscious holds the *samskaras*, which we would translate as all our buried traumas. *Samskaras* can be loosely interpreted as impressions from the past, which produce a whole variety of thoughts, feelings and actions, the origins of which we may be totally unaware of. The power of *samskaras* is tightly linked with the whole concept of *karma* (*see Karma Yoga, p 31.*) The unconscious activity of *samskaras* adds to our general store of *karma*, or reactive actions.

Samskaras are the cause of many self-perpetuating emotional states. Often too they are responsible for the feelings of alienation, depression and loneliness which are so much a part of modern life. Many contemporary forms of therapy are taking into account the spiritual and recognizing that the law of cause and effect has deep meaning for us on a psychological level. These accumulated 'samskaric scars' can be rooted out by extra awareness and self-observation. Ultimately, using yoga's techniques of going beyond the 'small self', they can be transcended, as we cease to identify with them and become part of a truer reality.

MAYA

The impressions which we harbour deep within the psyche can also cause many false illusions. The Sanskrit name for illusion is *maya*. In cosmic terms *maya* is the whole of the 'unreal' universe, the one which is subject to change. According to this philosophy, the mistake most of us make is to live as if this – the material world, including our own body and mind – is the real one. We attach to it all our hopes and dreams, our expectations and longings. When it fails us, as it often does, we are plunged into disappointment and despair.

Yoga teaches as a primary principle that this false identification is the source of our pain. Once we begin to recognize 'something else' is at play, and focus our inspiration on that, we have a chance to live in a more fulfilled way. Two major leaps are involved. We have to see illusion for what it is and stop acting as if it is real. Then the aim is to connect ourselves with what is ultimately more real.

This is not just a high-minded ideal. Like all yoga's precepts, it has validity even in the mundane world. At quite a simple level, we can see how lives can all too easily be based on illusion. One classic example is when we reproduce emotional situations from the past. A woman from an abusive home may marry a man who beats her. Here she is reacting to adult relationships as if they were those from her childhood, subconsciously choosing to get involved with the same type of characters even though she thinks they are different. Similarly, a man may overreact to someone who reminds him of his mother. He knows she isn't, but his emotions are giving him the false information that she is. In both cases these adults are not relating to current relationships, but are behaving as if the shadows of the past are present reality. Time and again we act under the illusion that we are aware of all the facts in the clear light of day, when in fact we normally extract from a situation what our *samskaras* tell us to, involving us deeper and deeper in a distorted world view.

MOKSHA

Yoga's answer is to liberate not only the emotions, but the spirit too. *Moksha* is the yogic term for liberation. In its broadest sense it means release from the cycle of death and rebirth, when we have ceased to cause more and more effects for ourselves and others to deal with. When we are in a state that no longer involves inappropriate reactions based on old emotions, we become free. This state of liberation is known as *nirvana* in Buddhist terms (the extinction of everything involving the ego), *samadhi* in the Hindu world, and to Westerners, world enlightenment. *Samadhi* is an ultimate merging, a state of oneness, the deep bliss of the mystic. It happens when all the groundwork of yoga has been done; psychologically and physiologically there is no trace of disturbance. Only then can one live in full spiritual consciousness.

TAKING THE JOURNEY

Thus yoga's spiritual journey is basically a progressive one, from an unenlightened state into a fully conscious one. This is not to deny the reality of 'spiritual' experience along the way. We would hardly be able to aspire to any kind of spirituality if we weren't capable of sensing its existence. Many of us can remember moments of 'peak experience' when we seemed to be living on a more intense level. What yoga attempts to do is to make this fully conscious state a more permanent part of our lives. Once there, we can no more be swayed from it than we could go back to being small babies.

Theoretical ideas are no substitute for transformational experiences. But in the yogic scheme, knowledge carries its own transformative power. And it helps to start a journey with a map.

Despite the unfamiliar models and terminology it employs, yoga's truths are basic truths. Our collection of ideas from the past prevent us from seeing clearly and keep us attached to the things that make us suffer. We repeat the same old mistakes, stuck in our emotional dramas, lost at the mercy of temporary ups and downs, feeling out of control. We identify with this turbulent life as if it is all there is, not stopping to realize that something far more peaceful is both 'out there' and within the depths of our own psyche. But once we start to realize that the 'waves' are of our own making and within our control, we can begin to calm our own storms and sense the placid rhythm that lies beneath.

Most of the time we fail to see the whole picture, one that includes the vantage point of permanent equanimity. But it is possible for us to move towards other realities. Observation, discernment, and self-control can give us the tools to get to a more spiritual place. Then – whether we choose to call it a heightened awareness, or a sense of connection, or an all-pervading peacefulness – it is ours.

PART 2

THE PRACTICALITIES

5

YOGA FOR PEACE OF MIND

USING YOGA'S WISDOM

Peace seems to be one of the most sought after, hardest to find commodities. And we should not think that this is just in our modern, harassed world. Life has always involved stress, or the sages of old would not have been inspired to find ways out of the pain it causes. I have described in previous chapters how the yogis and philosophers evolved a highly structured framework to describe the way the universe was set up. We – our minds, thoughts and activities – all have a place in that structure. But yoga does not just provide a neat, detailed explanation of why things are as they are. It gives us a variety of practical means for living life in an effective and transformational way. After all the theory, this second section of the book will deal with practical ways and means of reaching our highest potential.

Yoga is predominantly a system for living. Many people go about their daily lives doing jobs, relating to others, fostering world views in ways that are distinctly yogic. One thing that makes yoga so user-friendly is that you can do it without knowing any of its theories. Yoga is not a set of dogmas and practices just for the initiated. It has a sort of in-built elasticity just like the elasticity it aims to engender in the people who practise it. You will probably find as you read that some of these practical methods sound familiar. You may well already be doing similar things, or thinking along similar lines. So yoga is really an all-embracing world view, universal in its application.

The yogis of old had nothing less on their agenda than expanding their consciousness and achieving transcendental bliss. These, however, are not the first objectives in the minds of people who turn to yoga. The possibility of becoming more relaxed and of staying peaceful amidst daily stresses elicits more enthusiasm. In fact, the peace of mind that yoga promises is a considerable step towards transcendental states because the 'thought waves of the mind' are a major impediment to transcendental progress.

I will now look at how this peace of mind can be engendered. Patanjali's method, an assured, systematized route, is the one most closely followed. It is included here, but so are others from the whole gamut of yogic practice. Read them through, decide what appeals to you, consider your lifestyle and what is practicable. It may help to plan whether you will practise alone or with someone else. If you can find a friend or a group to share the path, then do. Your yogic meetings need not include physical postures at all. Instead you can discuss the concepts, and apply them to the many practices suggested here. You can remind each other of your aims, exchange experiences, feed back how you think you are doing. Some of these practices can be carried out as you go about your ordinary life, some require you to take 'time out'. But there is only one way to get results – don't just read about them, do them!

BASIC RULES

Yoga lays down guidelines for life. Yoga's 'ten commandments' are one of the earliest codes of ethics. They cover all the things we know to be correct and several more besides. In our society there are plenty of experts on practical matters, but after leaving school we do not hear much about rules and regulations. Ethics and self-discipline, behaviour and attitude of mind can seem outdated concepts in an age of individual freedom. However, research shows that when children are given rules they are happier and better adjusted. As adults we also require a little regulation in life; this is one reason why many people feel comfortable living according to religious precepts.

The yoga code is not there to make us feel guilty. It is fairly straightforward and taking it seriously brings rewards. Yoga ethics encourage us to re-examine what we are doing with our lives. It is not just a matter of doing the 'right' things. The basis of these ethics are universal principles, which can give us direction, so we do not live on whims. Through these we look at our inner impulses, so that hearts, minds and actions are as one.

The yoga *yamas* are the moral restraints. Non-violence is the first, referred to in Sanskrit as *ahimsa*. This does not just mean restraining yourself from physical violence; more difficult is the concept of non-harmful thought and speech. It requires great discipline to resist the temptation to gossip about someone else's faults. Thinking ill of someone is even harder to catch – you only have to be driving a car to note how many other road users you silently curse. We can understand how words may get across to someone and cause unnecessary hurt. But are thoughts as important as words? The thought itself has an impulse, a life force. It is in effect as active as the spoken word, and carries its own power. Watch what happens when you encourage yourself to have pleasant, understanding thoughts about others. Even in mundane circumstances – waiting in supermarket queues, taking rush-hour trains – see how the kind of thoughts you have affect your interactions.

The second restraint is honesty, or *satya*. There are many levels of deception. Are you being true to yourself? Can you live in accordance with your deepest beliefs? Are you covering up your real emotions in front of others? Observance number three is not stealing – *asteya*. Not just in the obvious ways, but are you taking someone's time? Are you violating their generosity? Fourth, *brahmacarya*, means chastity. Interpretations vary as to its exact meaning. At its most rigorous it can mean strict abstention from sexual relations, even including sexual thoughts. Even in the more liberated traditions of *tantra*, chastity meant that sexual activity was to be used for spiritual purposes. The general interpretation is that sex should not be a purely greedy, sensuous experience. Chastity can also be interpreted as the male deliberately not ejaculating in order to keep the vital energies circulating.

The final observance is non-covetousness, *aparigraha*. Do you cast a jealous eye your neighbour's new car? Do you wish you had the seeming good fortune of your friends? Is it always 'just your luck' that it pours with rain when you set out on holiday? The 'not fair, it always happens to me' attitude is not conducive to peace of mind. It keeps you chained in a state of embattlement against yourself and others. And when you really look, you will see that despite appearances, even the 'have-it-all's' aren't necessarily any happier than you.

Carrying out all the yogic *yamas* may seem to require placing considerable restraints on what appear to be natural, involuntary processes. But these are precisely the kind of primitive responses which yoga tries to check, in order that we be free of them.

The next five disciplines are called the *niyamas*. These are more concerned with inner attitudes than with those directed towards the outside world. First is purity, or *shauca*. This includes cleanliness of the physical body, both internal (through the yogic cleansing practices, *see Chapter 8: Yoga for Cleansing and Purifying*) and external, as in bathing and wearing clean clothes. Purity also extends to the heart, in whatever ways you interpret that – kindness, decency, warmth, generosity to yourself and others – all come under this heading.

The second of the *niyamas* is contentment – *samtosha*. Being satisfied with what you have presents enormous difficulties in a consumer-driven society. Can you go against the grain, settle for less rather than more? Can you genuinely count the good things in your life, and build on that sense of personal gladness rather than relying on the newest thing to make you happy?

Number three, *tapas*, is personal asceticism. This entails giving up all the extraneous things of life that take you away from your aim, whether they are of a mental or physical nature. Directing yourself towards the correct goal, without distraction or interference, isn't always easy. How often do we get put off by people around us, by our own negative thoughts, by immediate pleasure or long-term laziness?

Study, *svadhyaya*, is the fourth *niyama*. It implies intense involvement in both study of the self, and an exploration of the spiritual journey. Last comes surrender, or dedication – *ishvara-pranidhana*. Can you take on board the wider view of your life and its meaning? Can you stop wanting to know immediate answers, and trust to the process as it happens? Can you feel assured that everything is being looked after, that there is a purpose? Letting go is a primary principle of yoga. Once we can surrender to the moment, knowing we are doing all we can and that we are also involved in something far greater than ourselves, peace of mind follows.

A DEEPER KNOWING

We can gain more peace in our lives through knowledge. But, in the spirit of *jnana* yoga, the yoga of discovering the truth, it has to be a felt knowledge, the wisdom that comes from understanding. To reach this point we have to be in possession of the facts, in all their detail. It is no good making it up as we go along, being swayed here and there by whatever is currently socially and politically correct. Yoga's wisdom, though it may stem from a different place and culture, embodies eternal truths. Strange things happen when we begin to study it. We start to see correlations in our own lives, supporting in practice what we learn. It may be, for example, that we gain a deep awareness that there is some sort of eternal, unchanging quality within our lives, beneath the daily shifts of mood and activity, connecting us with a real sense of who we are and what we need. Science is also coming up with theories which bear strong resemblance to what the yogic seers knew. However we gain knowledge about our world, the important thing is to make that knowledge a part of our lives and enable it to change our outlook.

We can gain wisdom from many areas. The yogic scheme sets out a clear framework for our understanding. In the higher, universal worlds we can look at unity and wholeness, non-attachment and letting go. In the psychological world, we can study conditioning and false illusion, and cultivate self-knowledge and awareness. Then we can look at the interface of science and spirituality in the modern world.

OUR OWN WORLD OF UNITY

How can we appreciate that a wider, unified world really exists? Start by watching small examples of the unified consciousness manifesting itself in everyday life. Watch how, if you are with someone for a length of time, you start to act in synchronization. One of you voices something the other is already thinking. You may feel fully aware of what she is feeling without her talking about it. Maybe you express the desire for an obscure book. Without knowing about it, a friend visits you carrying the very book you wanted. A common occurrence is when you have a strong image of someone you haven't heard from for ages. The next moment the telephone rings and there he is. There are many examples of this — a blurring of the edges between what we think of as isolated entities: thought, feeling and action. We can call this intuition, psychic awareness, messages from the unconscious. You can practise becoming more sensitive to them. They are signs of the existence of a far more comprehensive energy field than you ever imagined.

LETTING GO – WITH LOVE

How can we practise non-attachment when everything seems to cry out for us to get attached to it? Our friends and families, precious objects, homes, places of beauty... The suggestion that we should be able to give them up, just like that, implies we should be callous and cut off from our feelings. How can we be loving and involved, yet able to let go of the most core essentials of our lives? The trick is to encourage the sense of balance which yoga is so famous for. This comes across in many different guises, from the headstand to the central, righting force of *sattva*.

So the object is not to become cold and detached but rather to effect a *real* involvement, in the light of the knowledge that everything is temporary and you never know when the universe will require you to move on. The most obvious example is death. We live our lives as though they are going to carry on for ever. We plant our gardens expecting to see the fruit of our labours in years to come. We do the shopping knowing what we will eat for Sunday lunch. We try to make our world as secure as possible, yet the one thing that never figures in our plans is the only one overriding certainty – our own death.

In fact we may 'die' many times in one lifetime. Moving house, being burgled of cherished possessions, leaving a job we have had for years. Getting divorced, changing partners, friends and family leaving us, going to live abroad. All these major transitions cause us to cut off and live new 'lives'. Once the transition has been made, it is surprising to see how quickly we adapt. The point is that we can and do let go, no matter how involved we were. We see that we can live without whatever we thought was indispensable.

Living 'in the light of leaving' like this does not make us less ready to live wholeheartedly. In fact the opposite is true. We tend to put more passion into life when we know it is only for a limited period. Look how much you can put into a holiday when you only have two weeks. See how terminally ill people go off on world cruises, determined to make the most of their time.

Yoga teaches us the lesson that what we have may be very important to us at the time, but we need not become dependent on it. In the ultimate scheme of things it isn't everything. We may even wonder why we were so sure we could only be happy if we had this or that in our lives. If we take this wisdom to heart, we find ourselves less afraid of loss, and more secure, adventurous, fulfilled and truly alive.

UNDER AN ILLUSION

How can we start to see the reality behind life's illusions? What we were told about the world and about our selves is often just other peoples' views. Our parents and teachers were themselves indoctrinated by a certain world view, and it is practically impossible for them not to pass it on. So our view of the world is often like seeing through a glass pane that becomes more and more distorted.

Yet we all seem to have been born in a state of clarity. Some people can remember distinctly knowing as children that what they were told was untrue. Sometimes families are deliberately withholding the truth, in the hope their children will be happier that way; sometimes they themselves are unaware of the depth of their own deception. Our aim as adults is to return to that childhood clarity, to learn to trust our own judgements.

Falsity comes in several guises. There is our false perception in universal terms, about the reality of the material world and its distance from the spiritual. Then there is what we want to believe about our lives, our capabilities, who we really are. Witness the changes that can occur when people start to believe in other realities. Often this happens through therapy. We can move away from our frightened self, our low self-esteem, our insecurities. We can achieve much just by looking at our own inner attitudes.

AWARENESS

Awareness is the key to getting away from these illusions. The more we watch, the more we start to put a gap between the self we have been identifying with, and the observing self. The 'observer', detached from this close identification, begins to see that instead of being 'a nervous person', they are just holding on to the idea of having 'nervous' energy. Perhaps the only cord binding them to this energy is the fact that their parents were nervous, or that they were told the world is a dangerous place. It does not have to have anything to do with their real, core selves. It's just an idea they have become so stuck to that they feel they are stuck with it. They do not realize there is a 'real' Self deep in there, who knows nothing about nerves.

Think about how many 'energy systems' you have running in your own psyche. They are magnetic things, these emotional energies. They run the world; you only have to watch how we behave to each other in families, businesses, politics. If we look closely, we can recognize that the emotional responses we have within us are clearly reflected in the external world. If you want to change anything that goes on 'out there', sages say the best place to start is yourself. So note what is at play as you relate to and interact with other people. And, when you locate something that seems horribly familiar, but which you really do not like at all, just watch. Know you 'are not it', no matter how long you have felt it to be part of you. It's just a temporary attachment, without which you can live far more effectively.

Tracing these things as if they are separate systems encourages detachment, but this time in the correct sense of detaching yourself from the unreal. Many spiritual paths emphasize this importance of remembering the underlying self, which existed before all these conditions and attachments. The more we realize what we are not, the more right we feel. And the closer we become to who we are, the deeper our sense of relief and peace.

SCIENCE CATCHES UP

For centuries the world view of the mystics had to go underground, derided by scientific realism from Newton onwards, which posited a fundamental separation between the different elements in the universe. Now, however, that view is being challenged by quantum physics, which returns to the world of mystical experience where reality is comprised of interrelationships and fusion. Einstein's theory – that everything exists against one force field – sounds remarkably familiar to yogic thinking.

The difference, however, is that the yogic practitioner actually experiences this unity by identification with it. Thus what remains a theory to Western science is an attainable reality in every fibre of the yogi's being. One feature of this experience of the unity of all things may be the blurring of the barriers between senses. A piece of music may be 'seen', for example, as a stream of colours. You may become acutely sensitive in your body, able to 'feel' what has happened in the past in a particular place. There is an intense sense of the breaking of boundaries, of energy releases, and, ultimately, of peace.

JOYFUL CELEBRATIONS

Why are celebrations such happy occasions? Even if we ourselves are not the cause of celebration, taking part in someone else's joy is an uplifting experience. Through celebration we can get closest to what is meant by the devotional bliss of *bhakti* yoga.

Give yourself as many opportunities as you can for celebration. Weddings, engagements, birthdays, anniversaries – all are good causes. Make parties, invite friends. Even death can be celebrated. We can be grateful for what the dead have given us, which lives on as a real part of our own lives. If someone has lived long and happily, let the funeral be a real celebration of their life, without discounting the sense of loss.

As you celebrate, forget about yourself. And you don't need alcohol to do this, even though all around you might be imbibing. Try getting to this state of mind without it. Yoga practitioners help themselves to good feelings without the morning-after headache. Next time, try the fully conscious route instead. Be open to other peoples' happiness, see how the general good cheer can wake up the genuine sense of joy that is within you. See how you can be really *present*, bringing out your warmth and love instead of your fear and defences.

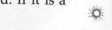

Be spontaneous – too much of the time Northern Europeans suppress their emotions, happy ones as well as sad. If it is a joyous occasion, let it sparkle. Even if you are usually a shy person, try looking beyond your inhibitions. Reach for your sense of connection with others, look for the place where you can genuinely relate from true feeling. Eschew social chit-chat if it means hiding the real you. Be yourself! Remember – bliss was never meant to be lukewarm.

The devotional route of yoga teaches us that we can use personal desire to build up that intensity of feeling. Do not be afraid to express the emotion of joy. Mediterranean people do it all the time. They are much better at celebrating than we are – look how their family events, meal times, meetings, are all causes for emotional outpourings. Remember, the spiritual path is not supposed to be all serious faces and meditation. We can show our gladness in being with one another, in other peoples' happiness.

Joy does not have to be linked with any particular occasion. Music and dance bring us onto another spiritual plane almost without us noticing. Do not forget to set aside time to listen to whatever 'turns you on'. Make time to go to concerts, try new sounds to listen to at home. As you do, concentrate in a new way. Do not listen with your old prejudices, try being sensitive to how the music is affecting you. Does it bring up images? How does it make you feel? Experience it not with your mind, but with your emotions. If it is a long time since you have played an instrument, take it up again. Be conscious of flowing with the music-making, without allowing your judgements of whether you are 'good' or 'bad'.

Maybe you have not danced for a while. Maybe you never dance at all. Try it now. Yes – you do not have to be 'good' at it. We make the mistake of not wanting to make a fool of ourselves all the time, so we leave the good feelings associated with the most natural, ancient ways of expression to those who we think can do it well. Why miss out on something so important?

Dance, as every young person knows, is a short cut out of 'mind stuff' and into sheer exhilaration. Again, it means you must disassociate yourself from feelings of 'I can't' and 'it's just not me'. Try it in the privacy of your own home; let go to how your body wants to move. Try local classes, do flamenco, jazz, jive. See how it can shake you into a totally different state of consciousness! The same goes for singing. So what if you have not got a 'good' voice? Singing is fundamental. Exercise those vocal chords, and let out your own sound!

WORK IT ALL OUT

Seeing your working life as a pathway to peace of mind might sound like the biggest transformation process in this whole book. But yes, it can be done. It's the basis of *karma* yoga, and one of the most accessible yoga paths.

Karma (*as explained in Chapter* 3), is essentially about the cosmic law of cause and effect. What we do sets other things off in motion. So *karma* yoga is about 'doing' in a conscious way, mindful of the effects.

To use your work well, there are two steps to bear in mind. The first is to become one with the 'doing', whatever the task may be. Think about how you usually do your work – and 'work' here includes the washing-up as much as investment banking. Is your mind a million miles away, wishing the task was over and that you were sitting watching television? Are you thinking about it, but agitated over it, angry at the problems, worrying that you aren't performing well enough? Are you letting it give you tensions in the mouth and throat, chest and arms? Are you subconsciously 'against' it, either actively detesting what you have to do or just bored by the routine?

Any of these feelings are likely to be part of our work experience. They all cause separation from what we are doing.

How would it be, then, to subdue the 'self' that has all these disturbing reactions? Think about the (probably rarer) occasions when you do something you enjoy: maybe icing a cake, planting shrubs, evolving a computer layout. What you experience is absorption. You feel completely involved in the task, almost 'in love' with it. Wild horses couldn't drag you away. This is a powerful experience of yogic 'union', where something 'higher' takes over from the small ego. You may feel as if 'you', with all your normal worries and tribulations, have disappeared. You and your job are one.

It is easy to talk about union with the things you love doing. But what about those you don't? Here it's just a matter of trying a little harder. You could start by forgetting your ideas about likes and dislikes. Usually, as soon as we approach a less than favoured task, 'anti' thoughts intervene. They set up their own processes – tension in the body, stress in the mind. Try to cut out the reactive response and go into your task without any associations. Maybe even consider finding ways to enjoy it. Take on a child's perspective, interested and innocent.

Now concentrate your attention on the task in hand, becoming thoroughly aware of each detail. If you are washing up, see how the detergent forms its bubbles. How many colours can you see in them? How fast does it cleanse a plate? What reflections do you see in a saucepan? By steady concentration try to be involved in the job, noting what occurs and letting go of any reactions. It may be possible to do this just for a matter of seconds at first. But catch how different you feel as you do it – more harmonious, more free. Gradually try to increase your attention span, and enjoy the easing pressure.

Linked up with this is the second part of the process – being unattached to personal gain. This is hard to come to terms with, because most of what we do is in the expectation of achievement. Doing something simply for its own sake is rare.

This does not mean that we do not try to do our best. But it is attachment to success, and fear of failure, that we want to avoid. If we do something purely for results, we miss the moment. The energetic impulse governing our action is a selfish one, and this will block its full effect at a spiritual level. It becomes merely a deed which begins and ends in our own desire. It also means that we are simply 'end-gaining' – looking to an imagined future and thus living in illusions and daydreams instead of concentrating on the 'now'. Even if things work out successfully and we reap the rewards of our actions, such happiness does not last long. Soon we start worrying about how long success can be maintained, and how to repeat it. The more we continue to achieve, the further we have to fall.

The solution is simply to keep yourself 'here and now', totally involved and staying present. Once you start to act in that way, the future does look after itself. You also grow more aware of what is the appropriate thing to do. If your work is making your life a misery, why not face it head on and find ways out of the situation? Admitting the truth will bring about its own changes.

'Doing' in the spirit of *karma* takes on a very different perspective. It becomes a spiritual path in its own right, here and now. As Krishna says to Arjuna in the *Bhagavad Gita*, 'Let thy actions be pure, free from the bonds of desire.'

6

YOGA FOR WAKING YOUR CONSCIOUSNESS

MEDITATING YOUR WAY TO SUPER-FUNCTION

Meditation can change your world. Some people also believe that it can change *the* world. Using it for relaxation, as we tend to do, is a rather limited application. Classically, the one and only reason for meditating was to arrive at supra-consciousness, a blissfully wide awake state. Relaxation is a prerequisite for this, but certainly not the end product. The Transcendental Meditation organization say that if enough people meditate at the same time, the consciousness of the planet will be raised, crime will disappear and there will be world peace.

Patanjali was the great exponent of the meditative process. As a preparatory stage, he advised sense withdrawal, or *pratyahara*. After this you proceed to concentration – *dharana*, contemplation – *dhayana*, and the meditative awareness of *samadhi*. Nowadays we tend not to demarcate these steps so strongly; we call them all 'meditation'. In fact they are not so much different techniques as different phases of transformation. Change becomes consistently deeper as you practice.

PRATYAHARA – SENSE-FREE

We live in a world of senses. Normally we set great store by having accurate and acute sensory responses. So why should we cut out these vital faculties? Because there are times when we need them, and times when they can be a distraction. Our senses are always drawing us into the outer world of material things. Often that is what we want, which is why we become television addicts or need constant background music. It is simpler not to look inside ourselves or at the non-material world. But once we want to go further, it is useful to be able to reduce the impact of the external world.

The power of the senses to distract us, even in ordinary situations, is easy to see. As I write, I am taken 'outside' myself by the noise of children at the school next door, people in the street, some distant construction machinery. All these induce different trains of thought – I go back to my own schooldays, remember I should visit my neighbour, wonder what the view of the new buildings will be like. As soon as I put earplugs in, physically 'turning off' the extraneous noises, I turn 'inward'. It becomes easier to think only about what I am writing.

The same thing happens with my sense of sight. During the day my eyes wander to the garden outside the window. Does the grass need cutting? How are those new plants doing? What shall I get next at the garden centre? When it gets dark, that world ceases to impinge. There is just me and the computer screen. This process continues if I smell something cooking downstairs. Yes, a snack would be nice, I'll just go and see what's happening... Or the cat wanders into the room. My instinct is to touch his silky fur, taking me away from the computer keyboard.

You will find *pratyahara* occurring of its own accord a lot of the time, but not under your conscious control. This is what happens when we are 'not there'. A child might be showing you something she made at school, while you are thinking about what to make for dinner. You will not 'see' the child's work at all, because your senses will be concentrated elsewhere. A friend may show you her new dress just after you have been visiting a sick relative in hospital. How much of the style and colour do you remember with your thoughts engaged elsewhere? We are adept at withdrawing our senses, but at random, rather than positively and at will. The trick of genuine *pratyahara* is to harness this ability and use it to good effect.

The most dramatic way of cutting external input is in a sensory isolation tank. You may be able to find one close to where you live. You float in warm water inside a dark, enclosed container. You are alone with yourself – the beating of your heart, the passage of your breath. It is a surprisingly pleasant experience. With no distractions, you feel everything within you becoming integrated. Peace and relaxation are the results.

You can try withdrawing the senses without any outside help. Start by tracing the many pathways your senses are following at this moment for you, as I did in the personal examples above. Then consciously draw them back, as if they were antennae. Instead of following the line of sight outwards, start with where it rests and imagine you are pulling it in through the eyes. When you hear a sound, allow your auditory apparatus to retreat from it instead of being drawn towards it. Feel as if you are leaving the sensory impression 'out there', with your senses retracted internally. To some extent, this will happen of its own accord whenever you are doing something complex. Your concentration takes over and your senses automatically cut out any stimuli.

Here is a very simple, classical yogic *pratyahara* exercise. Raise your hands to your face, resting your elbows on a table if you need to. Place your thumbs in your ears, your forefingers carefully over the closed eyelids (don't press!), your middle fingers on the sides of the nose (you may have to bend them), ring fingers over the nostrils and little fingers at the sides of the mouth. You should still be able to breathe lightly, if somewhat restrictedly. This exercise gently allows your focus to turn instantly within. You can do it any time you need to relax and shut out the outside world.

DHARANA – THE CONCENTRATED MIND

Once you have reduced your sensory load, you will find concentration comes almost automatically. *Dharana* comes from the Sanskrit 'to hold'. Attention is the thing being held. We all know what it is like to concentrate hard, but how long does that concentration last? What kind of concentration is it? Where does it lead and what are its goals?

Yogic concentration is on a different scale. It 'holds' for an indefinite period of time, not just a roaming, transitory thing, but under your control and available as and when you want it. And, whereas 'concentrating' in the normal scheme of things involves a tense, forehead-wrinkling, pencil-chewing effort, the yoga version is a free-flowing state of being, a direct contact involving far more than muscles and thoughts. It is an immediate forerunner to the meditative state.

You can practise *dharana* most effectively by focusing your attention on one thing. This is known as *one-pointedness*. In a way, it resembles the concentration we have when we are completely involved in what we are doing, except it is the concentrated *state* rather than the forceful act of concentrating. We usually have to make ourselves concentrate. Only after that may we fall into an active concentration, an invigorating state, where we are so intensely focused on one thing that we are oblivious to anything else. You often see children in this state of intense concentration, but as adults our consciousness is more diffuse. Yoga methods aim to achieve this state of total, relaxed focus – the real concentration.

The exercises that follow can be done alone or in pairs. You should first go through the instructions several times so that you familiarize yourself with them. Alternatively, you can take it in turns with a partner. One can read the directions as the other does the exercise. Another method is to make a tape of the instructions in the most appropriate way for you, allowing a suitable time between each one.

These concentration and meditation exercises may well help if you do them now and then, whenever you feel the need and have time. But if you really want consistent, life-changing benefits, there is no other way but to do them regularly. It is no good just reading about them and thinking about them. You have to set aside your own special, peaceful corner, tell everyone not to disturb you, close the door and begin!

PRE-CONCENTRATION EXERCISE

Choose the place where you will practise. It should be relatively quiet, with as few distractions as possible. Pick a time when you know no one will make demands of you, and make sure the answerphone is switched on or the telephone receiver is off the hook! Now sit in a comfortable position. It may be on a chair, on the floor, on a cushion. The main thing is to make sure you can keep your back straight without being distracted by discomfort, but don't get too comfortable – the aim is not to go to sleep!

Now close your eyes and take a few even breaths. Make sure you breathe evenly and deeply, without any force. Feel your rib cage moving gently, as well as your upper chest. As you breathe out, feel tensions draining away. On each out-breath, imagine your body becoming heavier and more relaxed. Be aware of any sounds that are going on around you, and withdraw your hearing from them. Be aware of any scents, and detach your sense of smell from them. Continue to breathe quietly, gently and evenly. Now you can go into the yogic *pratyahara* exercise, with your fingers blocking the organs of sense, as described above. Spend one minute on the exercise to start with, then gradually extend the time to five minutes. If at any time you start feeling tense and need to stop, do so. Don't ever strain to 'perform' yoga exercises!

To come out of your relaxed sense withdrawal, remove your hands from your face, and concentrate again on your breath. As you breathe in, imagine yourself becoming filled with fresh energy. Let the breathing continue in a relaxed, even way. Open your eyes. Note the fresh way you experience the things around you. Practise this exercise until you are familiar with it and feel it is having an effect. Only then go on to the concentration exercises.

CONCENTRATION ONE

First choose an object to concentrate on. It should be something fairly simple – a piece of fruit, a flower, a small ornament. Place it somewhere accessible; in front of you on the floor if you are sitting somewhere low, or on a table if you are in a chair. The object should be a little below eye level. Do the pre-concentration exercise described above.

Then, sitting in a comfortable upright position, blink your eyes rapidly a few times. Now flick your eyes from side to side – only move your eyes, not your head. Blink again. Now trace a circle with the eyes, alternately going clockwise and anticlockwise. Try to make the circle as wide as possible. Blink again. Close your eyes; rest the palms of your hands over your eyes. Take four even breaths. Open your eyes behind the palms, take the palms away.

Now gaze firmly at your chosen object. Ensure that your body stays comfortable and relaxed, and that your eyes are also relaxed, neither screwed up nor fixed wide open. Do not stare, and blink whenever you need to. Note without judgement everything about the object. The easiest way is to do a kind of internal note-taking – looking at the watch in front of me, for example, I can say to myself, 'White strap with seven holes, Roman numerals, black second hand', and so on. If possible, work from the outside of the object to the inside, trying to feel yourself becoming more involved in its 'heart' as you go on. Pay scrupulous attention to detail, as you would if you were drawing it. As I become more 'at one' with my watch, I see the delicate creasing on the strap leather, the exact way the minutes are delineated on the face.

In this exercise, try to recapture the innocent mind of the child, seeing something for the first time. We rarely see things with a fresh eye. You may think you know every aspect of your environment – now is your chance to find out how little the adult mind really experiences.

As you do this exercise you will find your mind wandering. This is exactly what normal minds do, so don't get too frustrated. The point is not to leap straight into a perfect state of unwavering attention. The idea is that you become aware of the mind's 'wanderings', and bring it gently back onto the object of the concentration. It is precisely this continual 'reining in' of the consciousness that creates the discipline. You become the owner of your own mind, instead of your mind dragging you wherever it wants to go.

You will find as you practise that your attention span does

increase. And the exercise will not just enable you to have an intimate acquaintance with a watch face or an apple. It will have spin-offs into daily life. You will find yourself more able to concentrate at work, in your social life, on learning sports or listening to lectures.

How long should the exercise take? Five minutes to start with. Try to set aside a regular time to do it each day, rather than just whenever you think of it. Assess the benefits you are getting in your own mind, and increase the time once you start getting results.

CONCENTRATION TWO

This time focus on something which is less 'fixed'. A candle flame, a drop of rain as it moves down a windowpane, a spider wrapping a fly in its web. Do the sense withdrawal exercises first. Then note the minute movements and changes of your subject, its colours, its direction. Try to prevent yourself becoming intellectual, asking 'head' questions such as 'I wonder why it's doing that?' or jumping out of the present with 'what's going to happen next?' These might be useful for the more intellectual *jnana* yoga, but not for the simpler 'mind skill' of concentration.

Now see the point at which the moving and the unmoving merge. The drop of water and the glass, or the mingling of one drop with several others. The edge of the flame and the air around it. See if you can cease looking at them as separate objects, and see them as part of one whole, indivisible picture.

CONCENTRATION THREE

This is a way of practising concentration outside in the world. Use your concentration skills consciously when you are out in the street, in the supermarket – anywhere at all. There is an old party game called Kim's game. Everyone stares at a tray of objects, which is then taken away. The person who recalls the highest number of objects is the winner.

This exercise is an expanded version of Kim's game. If you have ever wondered how people manage to find their way easily around strange cities, or report suspicious behaviour in detail, you can bet it's because they are good Kim's game players. They notice things – landmarks, architecture, car numbers. They are streetwise, aware of what is going on. This exercise is also the basis of the advanced driving test, where you have to demonstrate your continual awareness of road conditions.

However, for this exercise, instead of following your mind's comments, try to retain an open state of consciousness. Carry out the same noting process as before. This time, allow yourself to be aware of the whole object, simply noting what is there. Don't hold on to anything you know or feel about what you see. Just let it come into your awareness, then leave again as you go on to the next. This exercise will help control a 'scattered' mind, and eliminate the half-asleep state we tend to go around in. It will give you a sense of being awake, aware and alive in ordinary situations.

DHAYANA – THE CONTEMPLATIVE CONSCIOUSNESS

Contemplating has many connotations. It can be the contemplation of nuns and monks, the quietness and stillness of the ascetic. We sometimes refer to this jokingly as a sort of absence, when others look dreamy and far away. Yogic contemplation is a deep, yet subtle, state of unity. Once we become adept at controlling sensory input, and can concentrate the mind effortlessly, *dhayana* occurs. It is a direct result of this control of the senses, rather than something we can practice in isolation.

Being in *dhayana* is effectively an 'altered state'. Although 'different', it is also a perfectly natural state, where we are 'ourselves', but more so. It involves complete absorption and connectedness, and actually has nothing dreamy about it, but is rather a state of extraordinary awareness. You feel as if 'you' have disappeared and there is an unrestricted energy flow between yourself and the object of contemplation.

CONTEMPLATION ONE

This uses and deepens the experience described above of concentrating on a still object (*Concentration One*). When you have mastered the concentration process to your satisfaction, and are aware of the benefits it is bringing, you can take it a stage further. Probably you will have started to feel a deepening awareness and expansion anyway.

This time, after you have done the usual attentive noting, close your eyes and be aware of the internal after-image of the object. Stay focused on this image, its colours, its edges, until it fades. Then open your eyes and concentrate again, then bring the image inside again. Again, take care not to strain the eyes, and do a mental check of your body every now and then to make sure you are not tensing up. Continue with this process until you feel no sense of separation between you and the object. You should now be able to lift your focus from the original object, yet still feel the continued presence of integration.

CONTEMPLATION TWO

This requires a partner, preferably someone you feel completely at home with and who is also on the same journey of exploration. Sit comfortably facing each other and synchronize your breathing so you are both inhaling and exhaling together. Start by silently noting the person's appearance, hair and eye colour; all the exterior details.

Then gaze into each other's eyes, with the sense that you are losing yourself and becoming merged with the other. Try not to think consciously about the other person, or feel self-conscious. Let yourself 'get out of the way', as it were. If you find yourself coming out to a 'conscious' level, concentrate back on breathing together. Feel the sense of silent communion beyond intellect and senses. You may find you are intuitively sensing something about the other person, her emotional state, any physical pains or things from her past. You may experience these momentarily within yourself, yet know they do not belong to you. Check afterwards to see how accurate you were.

SAMADHI – MEDITATIVE UNION

The meditative state is a loss of self; an 'aliveness' and perceptiveness and a sense of deep connection. Your thought processes will feel stilled; not dull, but as if the thoughts themselves are receding instead of interfering. Rather than relying on the activity of the mind, there is an immediate knowing, a recognition of the truth about yourself and others. You feel 'in tune' with the universe and with your own being.

There should be no need to carry out any specific techniques at this stage. However, here are some of the more intense, powerful ways of getting into and maintaining the meditative state.

MEDITATION ONE

Sit in a relaxed, upright position. To check that the body is relaxed and free of tension, as you breathe in contract the muscles in each area from the feet up, then release all the muscles as you breathe out. Do the *pratyahara* sense withdrawal exercise if necessary. Close your eyes and sit quietly. Now imagine the loving presence of someone else, who cares or cared for you very deeply and unconditionally in the past. It may be a favourite aunt, a lover or a very good friend – someone who loved you exactly as you were. Try not to think of them as an individual, just allow yourself to sense their acceptance and support.

Now, as you breathe in, fill yourself with this feeling. You may see it as colour, or light streaming into you. As you breathe out, let the feeling, in whatever form it takes, circulate all around your body. Feel it filling and expanding you, becoming part of you. If you have any particular area of pain or discomfort, allow the feeling to travel there and warm and release it.

Now, as you breathe in, see the source of that love and feel as if you are growing so big that you can embrace and absorb it. Allow yourself and the feeling to become one and know that you are that pure self which was, is and always will be recognized and loved.

MEDITATION TWO

Sit as before and contract and release the whole body as in the previous exercise. Close your eyes, doing the *pratyahara* sense withdrawal if necessary. Now simply concentrate on the breath. Do not try to do anything with the breath. Just experience how it is, at this moment, for you.

Feel how the air is as it enters the nostrils, be aware of any constriction in either passageway. Trace the journey of the air, past the back of the throat, down into the lungs. Be aware of how the lungs inflate and deflate, and how their action moves the rib cage. Feel how much of the lungs are becoming filled, how much of the torso is involved. Be aware of any fluctuations in the breathing process, any internal restrictions. Keep coming back to the inhalation and exhalation, experiencing their rhythmic flow. Be aware that the process is happening involuntarily, without any conscious effort from you.

Now try to trace the impulse that keeps the breathing process going. Feel where it comes from, deep within you, this will to live. Note if any images come up as metaphors for this life force. Feel the deep point of changeover of the breath, from exhalation to inhalation, feel from where the 'in' breath arises. Be aware that despite your struggles and conflicts, your system knows it is part of the universal life force.

MEDITATION THREE

A sound meditation is often practised with a *mantra* (a word or phrase) that has been specifically provided for you. In its absence you can use the universal OM chant. Sit in a relaxed, comfortable way, as described above. The OM sound can either be repeated soundlessly and internally, whispered, or fully vocalized. The sound starts at the back of the mouth with an 'AU' sound, travels through to the front of the mouth with the 'OO' and is projected through the lips with 'MM'.

The sound should be accompanied with an 'out' breath. Pause to inhale gently and then coordinate sound and exhalation again. As you repeat the sound, imagine that you have a concentration of energy at the point just between and slightly above the eyebrows – the 'third eye' centre. As the sound leaves the mouth, focus on this point and feel it is connected to the totality of the OM. Then as you inhale, experience the sound throughout your whole body. Feel how it reverberates in the cavities of the head and vibrates through your arms and torso. As you exhale and make the sound, reconnect with the point of the third eye. Consciously experience the originating vibration of the universe and everything in it.

7

YOGA FOR STRENGTH OF BODY

PHYSICAL FITNESS FOR LIFE

Hatha yoga, the yoga which relates to the physical body, is the one most familiar to us. It consists of relaxation, breathing exercises and physical postures. It can make us supple and healthy, stretching muscles and building strength. It can help circulation and breathing, posture and hormonal balance. What is not so familiar, perhaps, is the way it affects a whole complex system of energies which we are not so aware of, the subtle *pranic* life energy of the body.

SUBTLE ENERGY – THE REAL LIFE FORCE

Modern science cannot find any evidence to verify the existence of subtle energy. Nevertheless, this energy is referred to in the earliest yogic writings, the *Vedas* and the *Upanishads*, and forms the basis of Indian and Oriental medicine. Acupuncture balances the flow of subtle energy through the system of meridians. In other systems it is known as *chi*, or *magna*. In the Hindu tradition it is called *prana*.

Prana is the underlying, basic life force found in all things.

It manifests itself in many different ways. All our body systems are under the influence of various forms of *pranic* energy. When the energy is unbalanced, not flowing as it should be, we are more likely to become ill. Therefore the correct functioning of this *pranic* energy is fundamental to our state of health and disease. Instead of looking at the external causes of illness, on which Western medicine concentrates, the yogic view is to correct the internal energy balance. Only then will we be strong enough to counteract the negative influences around us, such as bacteria and viruses, or emotional and environmental stresses.

By controlling this subtle energy system yogis also manage to perform seemingly impossible physical feats. They are able to slow the heart rate, to change body temperature, to defy conditions which would kill any normal human being. There are stories of yogis being able to remain for long periods locked in airtight containers or sit naked in the snow without any ill effects.

Pranic energy flows through channels in the body, very similar to acupuncture meridians. Ancient scriptures say there are between seventy-two thousand and three hundred thousand of these channels, or *nadis* as they are called in Sanskrit. However for most purposes we can talk about three principal pathways. The central one, called *sushumna*, flows directly up along the spine. To the left of this is the channel called *ida*, which is equated with a cool, moon-like force. To the right is *pingala*, the 'sun' energy. These two channels are not parallel lines. They criss-cross and intersect six times in their journey to the topmost point, the 'third eye' spot between the eyebrows. These intersection points are where the energy becomes most powerful – the *chakras* (*see Chapter 3, Yoga's Many Paths – Kundalini Yoga*). They are rather like signal boxes of the body, from which various 'lines' outwards are controlled. The *sushumna* current, however, is a direct pathway from the base chakra to the seventh point, the crown chakra at the top of the head.

Usually, energy travels somewhat randomly up and down the channels of *ida* and *pingala*. One of the aims of *hatha* yoga is to regulate this flow more consciously. It also makes the energy flow more directly through the central channel, where it can be available to the chakras. *Kundalini* yoga works specifically to stimulate a rush of energy through the *sushumna*. *Tantra* can also produce strong movements of energy through the central axis.

You will probably be unable to register the movement of these subtle energies, although sometimes we convince ourselves that we can. When you are practising yoga regularly enough, however, you will feel a sense of that life and energy. This is certainly one unmistakable way of experiencing the *pranic* force within us.

MORE THAN JUST A BODY

According to yoga, our physical body is just one level of a system of associated 'bodies'. You may have heard of the body's 'aura'; you may also have heard of its astral body and causal bodies. In fact it seems inconceivable that we do just stop at the skin, which in any case is soft, sensitive and highly permeable. Yogic writings say we extend outward into the universe in five levels, or *koshas*. Apart from the gross physical body, these levels are in the form of invisible sheaths. Each level is a kind of microcosm of the external cosmos. Thus everything which we think of as outside us is also within us.

The *pranic* force, flowing within everything, links the physical body with our other, more subtle, body layers. As we practise yoga we also extend *prana* through the invisible body. By reflecting on the wisdom of the body that we can touch and see, we can thus become more intimate with other levels of our own being and with the world outside us.

THE PHYSICAL NITTY-GRITTY

How does yoga affect us on a purely physical level? All the major systems of the body are influenced by *hatha* yoga practice. The muscular system is the one we are usually most aware of when we have been practising yoga assiduously. Even muscles you didn't know you had are involved. The yoga postures concentrate on a deep stretching movement. Unlike other forms of exercise, the muscles are given a gentle, controlled stretch, without any strain. They are thus able to extend gradually and safely. A flexible muscle is also a strong, well-toned muscle. If you see someone who practises yoga regularly you will notice that they have perfect development – not over-bulked or 'muscle-bound', but with a full range of movement. Regular practice will delay the ageing process by keeping muscles and ligaments moving. Although, as with any other exercise, you may experience muscular aches and pains after a yoga session, these will soon wear off, leaving you refreshed. Yoga should never make you feel jumpy or exhausted.

The skeletal system also benefits. As the muscles loosen and stretch, so do the ligaments which hold the bones in place. Instead of being held rigidly, under pressure, the bones become freed to move back into a more natural alignment. This is especially so in the case of the spinal vertebrae, as many of the yoga postures work directly on the spinal column. The postures are also preventative; they help guard against slipped discs, where the soft cartilage between each vertebrae has slid out of place.

The circulatory system improves through regular, deep breathing. Yoga helps you become more aware of your breath, even when you are not performing the specialized breathing practices. You are forced to use more of your lungs, and many of the exercises involve extending the rib cage, allowing more space for the lungs to extend. Oxygenated blood is pumped more effectively to all the organs, revitalizing them and carrying away toxins. The inverted postures enhance blood circulation, reversing the venous blood flow, and also improve lymph drainage.

The digestive system is helped by the internal massaging action which some of the postures perform on the organs. Twisting postures, and those which involve the back bending forwards and backwards, will help stimulate the digestive organs. The improved circulatory process (*see above*), allows cleansing blood supply to reach the stomach and intestines, and improves peristalsis. Doing the *asanas* will also make you particularly aware of your digestion! Any remains of a heavy meal will certainly be felt, and you will become more in tune with what your body needs to eat and drink and how quickly you are assimilating and eliminating.

The nervous and endocrine systems are affected. Yoga's concentration on the spine, through which the major nerve pathways flow, helps to control nervous energy. The nervous system is in some ways analogous to the flow of subtle energies referred to above. The spine is itself highly subtle and sensitive, and can be regarded as the closest material equivalent to the *pranic* channels. Regular yoga practice is well-known for reducing anxiety and panic states. Many people find that hormonal irregularities, such as menstrual problems, right themselves. Hyperactivity, as well as its opposite, lethargy, can also be overcome and yoga practitioners enjoy an even supply of non-draining energy. Emotions also become stabilized through doing yoga postures.

NOTE WELL!

There are certain practical things to bear in mind before you start doing any *hatha* yoga.

- If you have a medical condition, you should only train with a properly qualified yoga teacher, and consult your doctor first.

- If you are pregnant, do not start a yoga programme as a beginner. Consult a yoga teacher and only continue if you know exactly what you are doing.

- During menstruation, listen to your body. You may need to rest completely from yoga postures for the first couple of days. Do not do any inverted postures during your period.

- Do not eat beforehand – three hours for a meal, two hours for a snack.

- If possible, have bowels and bladder empty.

- Wear loose, unconstricting clothing that you can move freely in.

- Feet should be bare. The floor can be carpeted but make sure you can have a firm grip – no deep shag pile. On bare floors, practise the sitting and lying postures on a non-slip mat.

- Make sure the practice room is warm and that you are unlikely to cool down – have spare clothing to hand if necessary.

KEEP BREATHING!

Never hold your breath during the postures. The specialized breathing exercises are done separately, with simple breathing before a session and the more complex routines at the end. In the meantime, as you practise be aware of taking an inhalation before a posture, and exhaling as you go into it.

As you stretch and hold a posture, breathe as normally as you can, which may be somewhat restrictedly at times. Try to imagine yourself taking in energy with the in-breath, and allowing that energy to circulate around the body, especially to those areas which you may have trouble stretching. Always be aware of allowing the breath to come and go, without letting it become tense, even when the posture seems difficult.

HOME OR AWAY?

It is not easy keeping to any practice routine at home. On the other hand, it may be easier than dragging yourself out to a class on cold winter nights – or even on hot summer ones. But – and this is the part no one wants to hear – you do have to practise. You really will not get much benefit at all if you pick up this book every few weeks, try some of the exercises then put it back on the shelf and leave it there. It is regular and consistent practise that pays off. Even if you go to classes, it pays to supplement what you do there with some daily practice.

The good news is that you do not have to do that much. Dedicated practitioners will be up at the crack of dawn to make sure they get their practice in, but that is not for everyone. So make your yoga practice work for you. Make it into something you enjoy. Do it with a friend you would not otherwise get together with. Do it in office lunch hours, or make it a rule when you get back from work. There are only ten exercises listed here – that's a very abbreviated programme, which anyone should be able to fit into the day. The whole session should not take longer than 45 minutes. You will take more time on it at first, while you are learning, especially if you have never done yoga before. However, as you start to practise you will find you feel 'not quite right' on the days you do not do anything. Your body needs its yoga!

You may prefer to divide the practise up into separate times during the day. You can, for instance, do the warming up and the Cat pose first thing in the morning; the four standing postures at midday; the sitting postures at tea time; and the spinal twist and the shoulderstand before going to bed. That amounts to ten to fifteen minutes a session – which sounds far less rigorous. If you decide to practise in separate sessions, begin each one with the abbreviated relaxation, breathing and warming up exercises.

STARTING A SESSION: ONE – RELAXING

All yoga sessions should start with a brief relaxation. Lie on the floor, stretch your arms out to the sides, and your feet out. Wriggle your back around on the floor, easing any tension. Now bend your knees, with feet on the floor close to the buttocks. Take the back of the head in the hands, lift it slightly and ease out the back of the neck. Make sure the back of the neck stays slightly elongated as you replace your head on the floor, with the chin tucked slightly downwards. Replace the arms on the floor, at a 45 degree angle from the sides of your body, the palms of your hands facing upwards. Feel as if your whole spine is dropping towards the floor. Feel the contact of all the vertebrae with the floor.

Now stretch your legs out along the floor. As you inhale, gently contract and release each area of the body, relaxing as you exhale. Start with the feet, continue to the legs, buttocks, waist, torso, shoulders, arms, hands and fingers. Then the face. When you have finished, mentally check your whole body. See if anywhere still feels tense. Areas which hold tensions that are often hard to shift are the face, shoulders, stomach.

For an abbreviated relaxation, simply lie or sit, and contract the whole body on an inhalation. Now push the breath out of your mouth forcibly in a big sigh, and let go and relax the whole body. Do this three times.

STARTING A SESSION: TWO – BREATHING

Now you are ready to breathe. The essence of yogic breathing is very simple. It's just breathing completely, as you did when you were a small baby. Watch children or animals as they sleep – you will see exactly what deep, rhythmic breathing is. Now is your time to relearn it.

First stretch your whole body out in a deep, long stretch. Feel as if you are extending from the waist: upwards with torso, arms and hands; downwards with belly, buttocks, legs and feet. Now bend your knees again with your feet close to the buttocks. Place the palms of your hands over the bottom of the rib cage. The middle fingers should be just touching, an inch or two above the navel.

At first just be aware of how you breathe normally. Is the passage of breath restricted in any way? Are you using only part of your lungs? Is only your upper chest moving? Our breathing patterns are intimately connected to our emotions – so tune in to how you are feeling as you breathe, and how your feelings alter as your breathing pattern changes.

Now as you breathe in, feel the rib cage expanding to accommodate the full movement of the lungs. Try to fill the bottom portion of the lungs first, allowing them to swell towards the top. Then as you exhale, deflate the lungs from the top down. You should also be able to feel the movement of the abdomen, and the fingers should gently move away from one another on the in-breath. Continue with this rhythmic rising and falling, allowing the breath to feel easy and unrestricted. In particular, do not try to breathe in or breathe deeply. You will find that if you concentrate on the exhalation, allowing it to be as complete as possible, the in-breath will come of its own accord. Trying to 'do' deep breathing will only result in strain. In fact, tension is mostly connected with a sharp indrawing and holding of breath, and inadequate exhalation. So breathing in may compound the problem. You simply need to be able to breathe out to let go.

Do this for ten inhalations and exhalations. Then allow yourself to return to natural, normal, relaxed breathing. Stretch out again.

For an abbreviated breathing session, simply sit or lie still with eyes closed, and become very aware of how the breath is flowing. Consciously take three breaths using the lungs to the fullest, feeling the movement of abdomen and rib cage.

STARTING A SESSION: THREE – WARMING UP

Always warm and limber your body before you start the proper exercises. Make sure you are on a carpet or thick mat at this stage. If you have nothing else suitable, lie on a folded blanket. After breathing and stretching out, wriggle your body around on the floor. Press the back down, and the small of the back, trying to eliminate the hollow. With the knees bent, raise your bottom off the floor, keeping the back of the neck as flat as you can. Now curl the spine back down on the floor, starting with the top and pressing each vertebra down one by one until the small of the back is resting on the floor. Repeat twice.

Bring the knees into the chest, hugging them with your hands and keeping the back of the head on the floor. Then start to rock gently backwards and forwards on the floor, with the back rounded, this time lifting your head as you rock forwards, while trying to lift your bottom off the floor and roll onto your shoulders as you rock back. As you rock, feel as if you are massaging the spine. Now see if you can speed up the momentum so you come to a standing position – preferably without using your hands! The way to do this is to make sure you rock far enough back onto the shoulders, then roll right forwards, placing your feet as close as you can to the buttocks. If this is too difficult, instead simply rock gently from side to side then get up carefully.

As you come to your feet, bend forwards from the waist and hang with the feet about a hip's width apart. Allow yourself to feel loose and floppy. Let the back of the neck relax and the tension ease out of the shoulders. Move the shoulders and the torso around a little and let the head hang – this is not a rigid position. Keep the arms and hands released. Now come up gradually. Uncurl the spine, as if you are resting one vertebra on top of the other. Keep the arms and hands relaxed. Let the head stay relaxed and bring it up last of all.

Now you can begin to limber the whole body. Start with the head – gently move it from one side to the other as if you are trying to get each ear to touch the shoulder. Feel the muscles stretching on either side of the neck. Move slowly and carefully three times to each side. Now gently allow the head to fall back, opening the mouth. Bring the head back to the centre, then let it come forwards, with the chin towards the chest. Do this three times, finally bringing the head upright and facing forwards.

Now raise both shoulders to the ears, allowing them to relax as they fall. Do this three times. Next shake out each arm, giving it a really good shake until you feel the blood circulating fully and the hands becoming warm.

Then, with feet further apart, swing your body round from the waist, allowing your arms and head to follow the movement round. Bend your knees each time you swing to the back. Feel the body getting warmer. Make six swings to each side. Then shake out each leg, and each foot, until they feel very loose and floppy.

Finally, stand once more with the feet your hips' width apart, feet parallel and toes pointing forwards, and close your eyes. Place the weight firmly over both feet, so you are resting neither on the ball of the foot nor the heels. Allow the legs to be firm and feel solid, with the kneecaps lightly drawn up but not rigid. Feel as if you are creating space around the midriff; that is, between the lower rib cage and the hips. Allow the spine to feel relaxed but erect, with space between each vertebra. Let the shoulders, arms and hands relax. Let the neck lengthen lightly, and the underneath of the chin be parallel to the floor. Imagine you have a string coming from the top of your head, attached to the ceiling. Stand with the eyes gently closed, try to feel light, yet solid and firm; breathe evenly and regularly. Enjoy the feeling of strength, solidity and balance.

Now open your eyes, relax your knees, stretch your hands upwards on an inhalation, and exhale through your mouth as you allow the whole body to flop forwards from the waist, allowing the knees to bend as you do so. (But be careful – If you have any trouble with the lower back, do not do this exercise.)

Now you are ready to start the 'Cat Pose', the final stage of

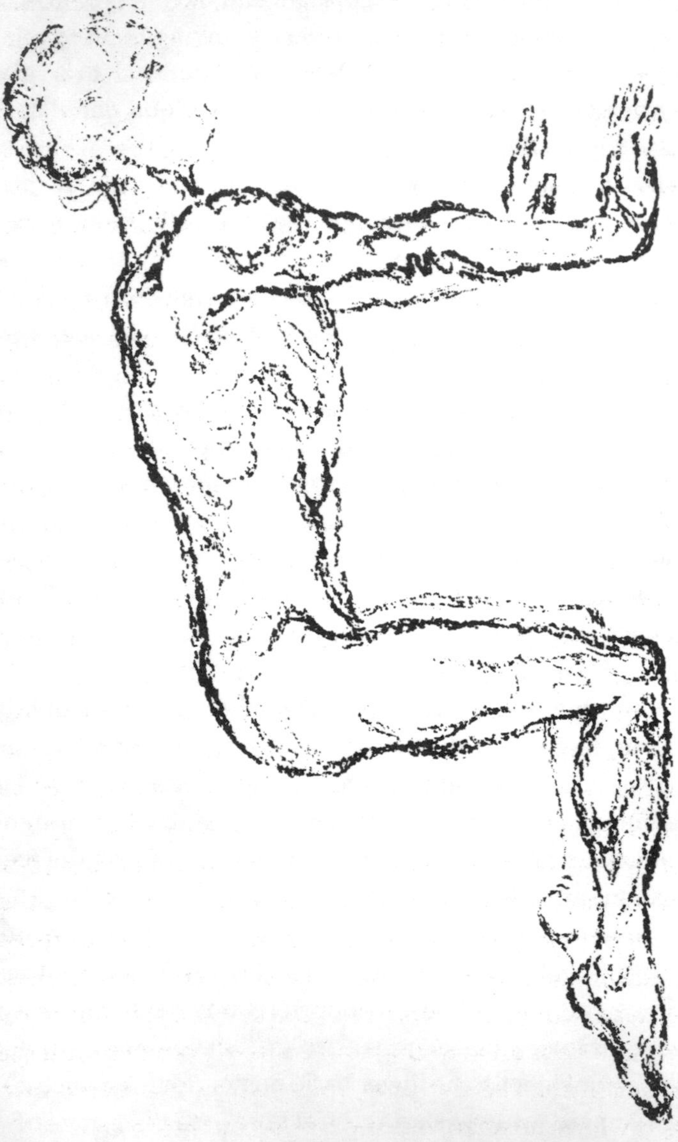

CAT POSE

your warming up session. Go down on all fours, with your hands on the floor directly underneath your shoulders, fingers straight out in front of you. Your knees are on the floor with the thighs at right-angles to the floor, the tops of the feet stretched out behind you. Take two even breaths in this position. On the next inhalation, raise the head as if you are looking up (coming up for air, as it were), and hollow the back. Try not to tense your shoulders. As you exhale, bring your head in, moving the chin towards the chest, and make your back round, bringing the belly up.

Repeat these movements, breathing evenly, coordinating your movement with your breathing. Try as you move to concentrate fully on the body, gradually extending the range of movement in the spine. Make this an exercise in concentration, as well as a physical one. If you find your mind wandering, bring it back to the body. Try to be fully 'present', with your mind in your body. Be aware of any places that feel rigid or stiff – it is normal for some parts of the spine to move more flexibly than others. Work on getting more movement into these stiff places rather than over-extending the places which are already flexible. Continue with the Cat pose for six inhalations and exhalations.

Finish by sitting back with your bottom on your heels, forehead on the floor, and the arms stretched out in front of you with palms facing down and forwards, elbows as straight as possible. Now clasp your hands behind the base of the spine, and gently ease yourself onto the top of your head, raising your bottom off the floor and straightening your arms, raising the hands out behind you with the elbows straight. Do this three times, sitting back onto the heels in between the stretches. Finally, relax with your bottom back on your heels, forehead on the floor, and your arms resting by the side of your feet with the palms facing up. The Cat pose, followed by this raised-arm stretch, can form an abbreviated warm-up on their own.

CONTINUING A SESSION – POINTS TO REMEMBER

As you undergo the physical practices of yoga, try to make them exercises in concentration at the same time. Tune into your body: what you are feeling, where you are stuck, where you move easily. Try not to allow your mind to wander. Of course it will, but become aware that this is happening and bring yourself back into a full involvement with the task in hand. Be aware also of your mental attitude to the practice – whether you try too hard; give up too soon; whether you are put into a negative frame of mind because of the difficulties; whether you see them as challenging or overwhelming. Each practice will be different – your body will be sluggish or responsive, your mind fresh or burdened. Simply be aware of all this, without judging it.

Physically, the exercises should certainly provide you with a stretch, but do stop at any sign of strain. The idea is to loosen any tensions, rather than put more in. The more you can relax into the posture, pushing just so much but not enough to create new stresses, the better your practice will become. Yoga is always about finding balance. In posture this becomes entirely physiological, a practical, kinaesthetic awareness which will spill over into all areas of your life.

The time you spend holding a posture will vary according to your own fitness and needs. If you are a complete beginner and not very fit, hold each posture for just one breath. As you become stronger and more adept, increase the number of breaths you take to a maximum of five.

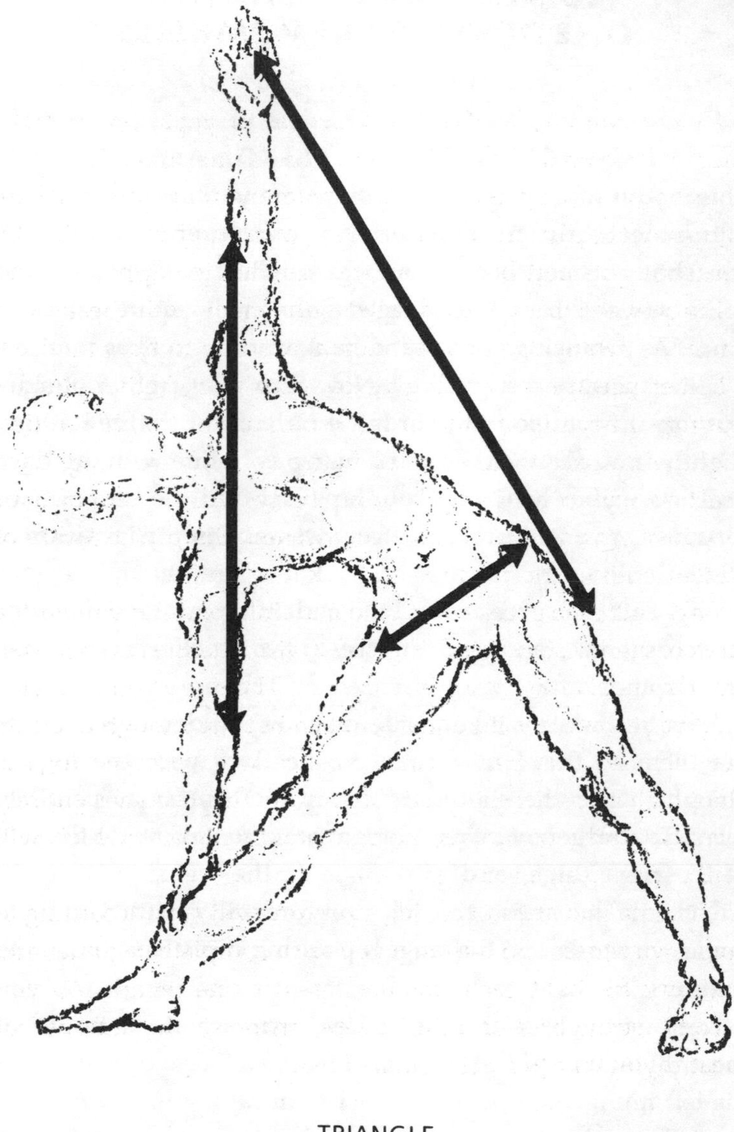

TRIANGLE
Thick black lines indicate direction of maximum stretch and main area of energy release

CONTINUING A SESSION: ONE – STANDING POSTURES

(Sanskrit names are in brackets)

TRIANGLE (UTTHITA TRIKONASANA)

This is your first classic yoga posture. Stand with your feet two to three feet apart; the exact distance will depend on your personal body proportions. If your legs are short you will need less space between them. Long-legged people will require more distance. As a quick gauge, stand in a way that makes you feel well-balanced and supported. Now turn your right foot sideways so the toes point towards the right and turn the left foot slightly inwards so that the left instep is in line with the right heel. Place your hands on your hips and turn the torso to face forwards. You will probably feel awkward in this position at first – don't worry. Try to keep the knees straight and the legs strong. Feel the space around the midriff by drawing the torso upwards while standing firmly. Try to avoid hollowing the base of the spine.

Now lift the arms gently sideways to shoulder level, stretching them so they are parallel to the floor with the fingers straight. Keep the shoulders down and, as far as possible, relaxed. Now gently lower the right hand so it comes to the side of the right thigh, and the whole of the left side is gently stretched. Then raise the left arm vertically, with the palm facing forwards and the fingers pointing directly towards the ceiling.

Keeping the legs straight, guide the right hand as far down the right leg as it will stretch, holding the left arm upwards and the left hip facing upwards rather than caving in towards the front. Then slowly and gently move up, and move both arms back into the sideways stretched position. Lower the arms and turn the feet so the toes are facing forwards.

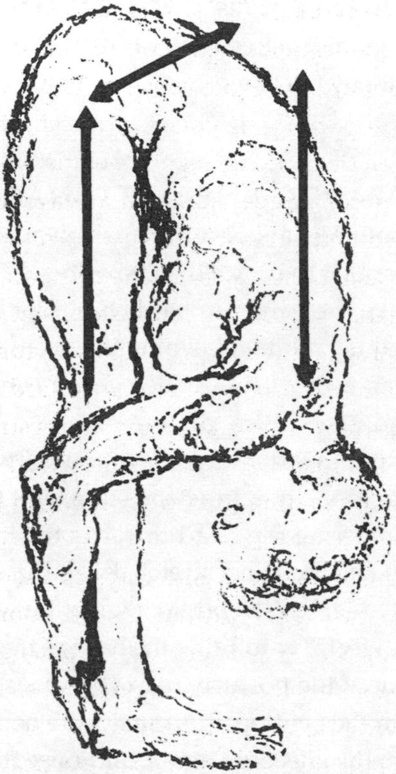

HEAD TO KNEE POSE

Shake the body out gently, from the feet to the shoulders and the face. Be aware of any tensions and relax them out. Then perform the Triangle posture to the other side; that is, with the left foot facing leftwards and the right turned in at a left angle. The arms come out to the sides, then the left hand goes down the left leg, the right is upstretched. Come out of the pose as before and shake out any tensions.

HEAD TO KNEE (UTTANASANA)

Stand with your feet about a hip's width apart, feet facing forwards and parallel to each other. Now bend forwards from the waist, and take the hands towards the floor, as far down as is possible without straining, keeping the knees lifted and the legs straight. Catch hold of the ankles if you can; if not, place the hands behind the calves or knees. Now, keeping the legs straight, gently draw the torso down and inwards towards the legs. Think in terms of taking the stomach towards the thighs rather than lowering the head towards the knees. In this way, the spine will lengthen and stretch. Keep the shoulders, back of the neck and the face relaxed, and keep the weight evenly centred over both feet. Try to relax the base of the spine.

To come out of the posture, relax the knees, arms and hands, and staying in the bent position shake the body around loosely. Now draw up the kneecaps again, and raise the torso gradually, with the head coming up last, as described in the 'Warming Up' section.

WIDE LEG STRETCH (PRASARITA PADOTTANASANA)

Stand with the legs between four and five feet apart, the toes pointing forwards. Draw the kneecaps up and straighten the

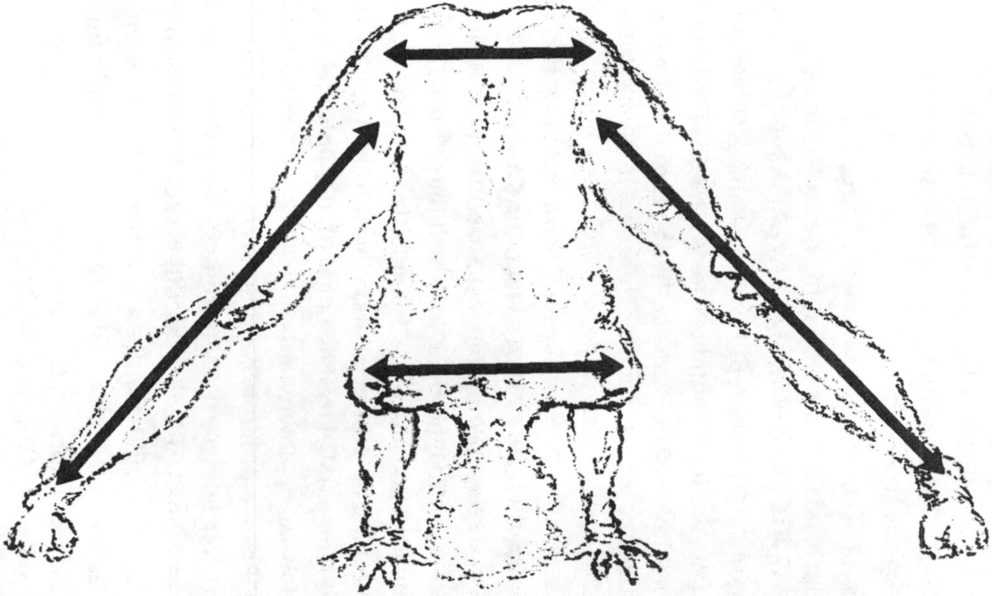

WIDE LEG STRETCH

legs, using the thigh muscles. Ensure your weight is evenly placed over both feet. Now lean forwards and place your hands on the floor in front of you, with the palms flat on the floor and the fingers pointing forwards. Then gradually walk the hands inwards as far as you can; ideally they will be in line with the feet, but as near that position as is possible for you. Do not sacrifice the knee and leg position!

To come out of the posture, allow the knees to relax slightly and walk the hands forwards. Shift the feet closer together until they are a hip's width apart, then shake the body loosely to relax it. Draw up the kneecaps once more and gently raise the torso as before, gradually building the vertebrae up, one on top of the other, with the shoulders and head, relaxed and hanging, coming up last.

WARRIOR (VIRABHADRASANA)

Stand with your feet four to five feet apart. Turn the right foot out so it faces towards the right, and turn the left in so it is facing the same direction, as in the Triangle. Turn the torso to face forwards, keeping the feet in position. Now raise the arms sideways so they are parallel to the floor, with the fingers extended and the palms facing downwards.

Keeping this arm position, bend the right knee and lower the right thigh. You may need to move the feet wider apart, but keep the same angle. Ideally the thigh should move so it is parallel to the floor, but try at the same time to keep the left leg as straight as possible. Look to the right, over the right fingertips. Keep the torso upright, the back straight and the arms up. The right knee should be kept above the right foot rather than caving in towards the front. Keep the shoulders down and relaxed. Keep breathing!

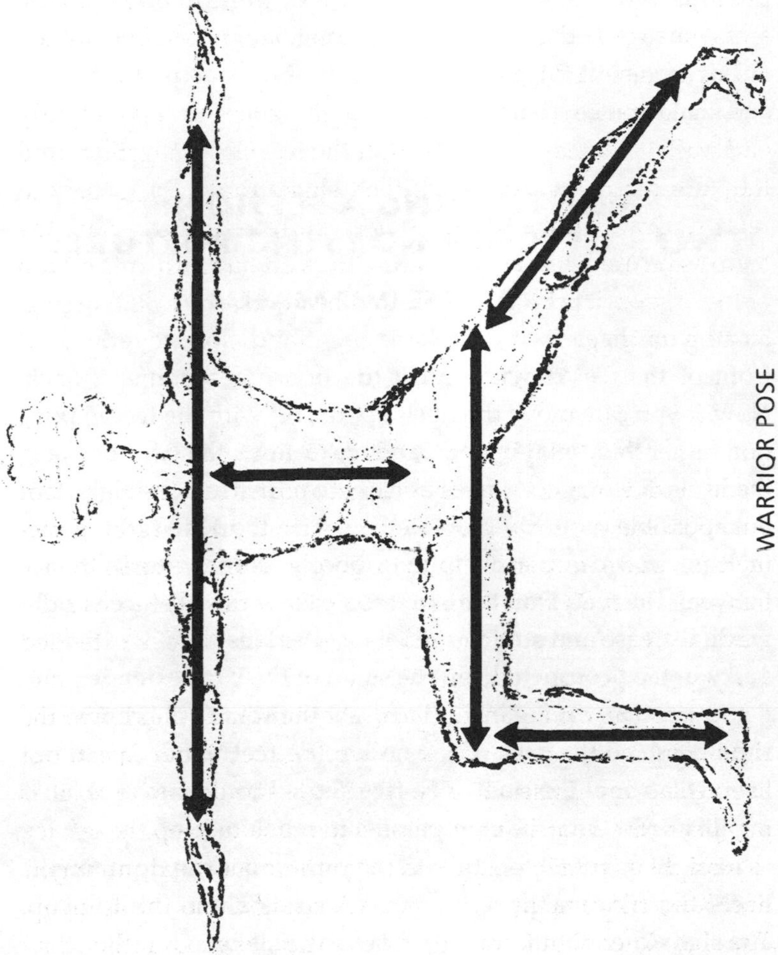

WARRIOR POSE

To come out of the posture, raise the right knee and straighten the right leg, face the front, lower the arms, relax the legs, move the feet closer to one another and shake out any tensions. Then repeat the posture to the other side, with the left foot pointing towards the left, the right foot slightly inwards, the arms outstretched, the left knee bending, and your eyes looking out over the left fingertips. Come out of the posture as before, and shake out any tensions.

CONTINUING A SESSION: TWO – SITTING AND LYING POSTURES

HERO POSE (VIRASANA)

Sit on your heels, with the knees bent and close together, the front of the feet down against the floor, toes pointing back. Now, if you can, move the heels apart, still with the feet in position rather than splaying out, and try to sit on the floor between the heels, keeping the knees as close together as possible. If this is impossible (which it may well be at first, due to tight ankles or legs), you can place a pile of books under your buttocks, between the feet. Don't make it too easy – the posture should gradually ease and stretch the legs and ankles.

Try in the posture to keep the small of the back extended and flat rather than caving in, and to draw the spine up, keeping the shoulders and the back of the neck relaxed. The hands can rest in your lap or at the sides. The face should be relaxed and looking forwards, with the chin parallel to the floor.

To come out of the posture, ease yourself back up to sit on the heels, then release the legs so they are straight in front of you, and shake them out loosely to relax any tension.

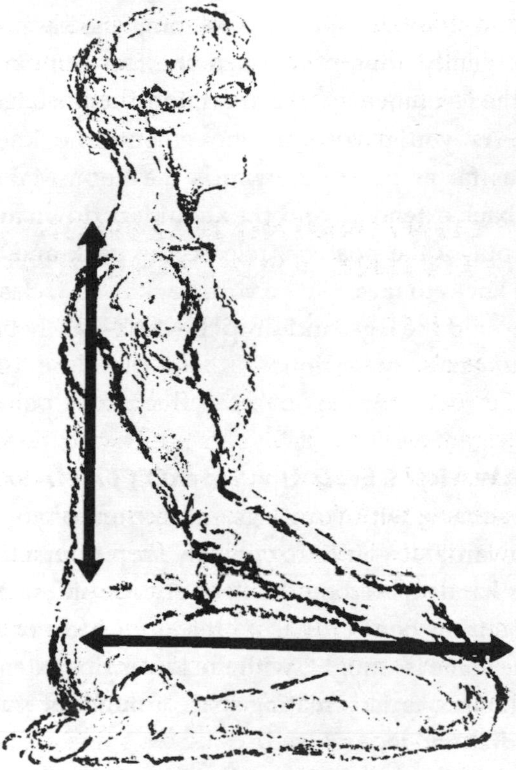

HERO POSE

COBBLER POSE (BADDHA KONASANA)

Sit with your buttocks on the floor and your knees bent out to the sides, the soles of the feet together and the heels as close in towards the perineum as possible. Clasp your hands around the feet, and draw the spine up, keeping the base of the spine flat. Now gently attempt to open the feet out, so the inside edges of the feet move further apart, the outside edges pressing together. As you make this movement, the knees should descend as far as possible towards the floor. Make sure you keep the back extended, and the shoulders down and relaxed. To come out of the posture, release the back and hands and allow the knees to raise. Make your back round, clasp the arms loosely around the legs, and drop the head lightly between the knees. Shake out any tension.

FORWARD BEND (PASCIMOTTANASANA)

Sit in an L-shape, with your legs out in front of you, your toes facing upwards. If you like, you can prop yourself up lightly with your hands placed on the floor at your sides. Try to sit up on your 'sitting bones', that is, the underside of the pelvis. Ensure the spine is straight, with the lower ribs extending away from the hip bones and creating space around the midriff. Keep the shoulders and face relaxed.

Now extend the hands down the legs as far as you can, without sacrificing the straight position of the legs. Ideally, the hands should be placed around the feet, or the index finger around the big toe. If you cannot manage this, it may help to have a tie, soft belt or thin scarf to hand, which you can hook around the feet, holding onto each end with the hands. Whether using the tie or your hands, the idea is to lever your torso gradually downwards over the legs. As with the Head to Knee pose, think in terms of the stomach coming towards the

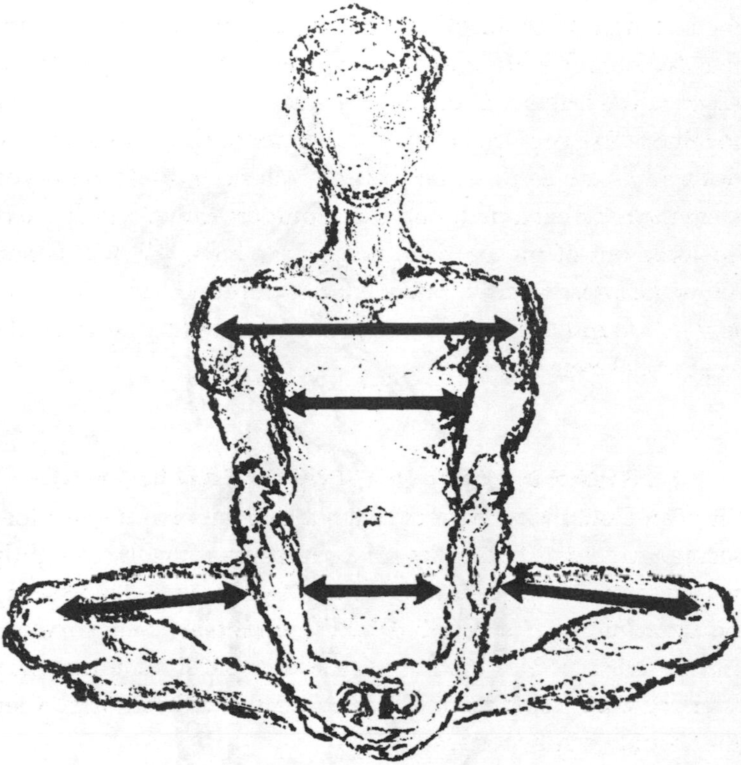

COBBLER POSE

FORWARD BEND

thighs and the spine gently elongating, as if you are making a hairpin shape. Do not drop the head towards the legs and let the back become round! Make sure all the time that the back of the knees are pressing down towards the floor, and the legs stay straight. Do not pull with the arms and shoulders. Breathe quietly and normally. Continue easing yourself down gently, visualizing the spine lengthening like a piece of elastic. To come out of the posture, release the hands or the tie, bend the knees slightly, and allow the torso to flop forwards. Shake out any tensions and wriggle the legs around.

COBRA (BHUJANGASANA)

Lie front down on the floor, arms bent, palms down in front of you on the floor with the forehead on the back of the top hand. Allow the toes to face inwards and the heels to flop apart. Release any tensions, particularly from the lower back.

Then place the hands underneath the shoulders, with the palms flat and the fingers facing forwards. The fingertips should be in line with the top of the shoulders, the elbows sticking out. Point the toes down so the soles of the feet are facing upwards.

Now gently raise the torso off the floor. Try not to rely on the hands and arms, although you may press lightly down on the palms. Keep the shoulders relaxed and the face looking down towards the floor. As you raise the top part of the body from the floor, concentrate on extending the spine and using the muscles of the back to do the lifting. Press the hips gently into the floor to give you more support. Continue to breathe lightly and as normally as possible. Avoid the temptation to strain the lower back or tense the shoulders. Do not worry if you can hardly raise the body. This exercise improves the strength of the back and this will come in time.

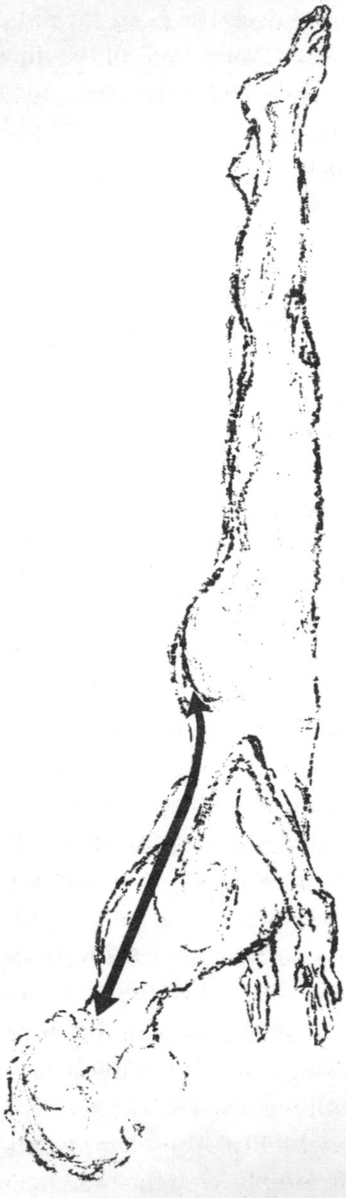

COBRA

To come out of the posture, gently lower the torso back to the floor, bend the arms in front of you again and rest one cheek on the back of the hands. Then go into the posture again, trying to lift a little further. Then lower the torso again, rest the other cheek on the back of the hands, release the feet and release any tension from the back.

CONTINUING A SESSION: THREE – TWISTING POSTURE

SPINAL TWIST (BHARADVAJASANA)

Sit on the floor and bend the left leg so the left foot turns inwards towards the right thigh, and your weight is slightly over onto the left buttock. Now bend the right leg, placing the right foot over the left thigh onto the floor. If you are unable to do this comfortably, you may extend the left leg and simply place the right foot flat on the floor outside the extended left knee.

Now try as far as you can to sit evenly on both buttocks, and to extend the spine. As in previous postures, feel as if the midriff is lengthening and the torso is lifting up out of the pelvis – try not to collapse in the middle. Place the palm of the left hand behind you on the floor by the buttocks. Using this hand as a lever, try to extend the spine a little more. Drop the right buttock by releasing any tension. Now straighten the right arm across the body, with the right elbow pushing against the inside of the right knee and the right palm stretched outwards towards the left. Using this right arm as a lever, turn the whole torso leftwards from the waist. Make sure you are keeping the spine long and upright. Resist any temptation to twist the neck and head to the left. Simply keep the head in line with the torso,

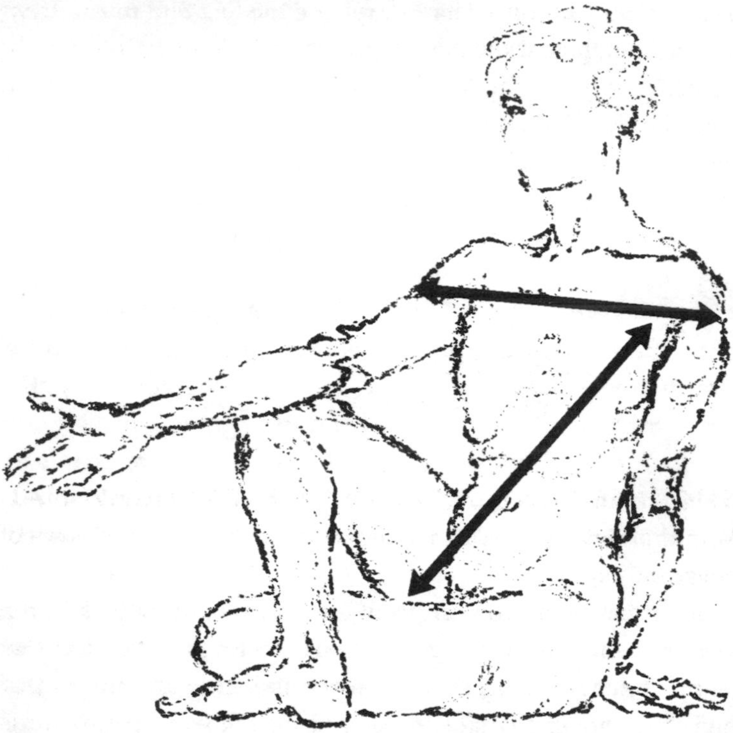

SPINAL TWIST

and turn the whole body from the waist, pressing down all the time with the right buttock. Try not to put tension into the shoulders. Breathe lightly and evenly.

To come out of the posture, release the arms, turn the torso back to the front, untwist the legs and shake them out in front of you. Then repeat the posture to the other side, with the right leg bent inwards, the left foot on the floor outside the right knee, the right hand behind you and the left arm coming across the body with its elbow levering against the inside of the left knee. Turn the whole body from the waist towards the right. Release, and shake out any tension as before.

CONTINUING A SESSION: FOUR – INVERSION

SHOULDERSTAND (SALAMBA SARVANGASANA)

Women should not perform this posture during the first days of menstruation.

Lie on the floor on your back with your knees bent. Lift the head in the palms of the hands to ease the back of the neck out gently. Replace the head on the floor, making sure the back of the neck is stretched and the chin pointing downwards towards the chest. Place your hands by your sides.

Now take the feet off the floor, and try to extend your legs backwards over your face, lifting your buttocks from the floor and rolling onto your upper back. You may support the buttocks or the small of the back with the hands. Gently ease yourself as far as you can onto the shoulders, gradually supporting yourself with your hands further and further up the back towards the shoulders. You may feel some constriction in your upper chest or throat. This should clear as you get more used to the posture.

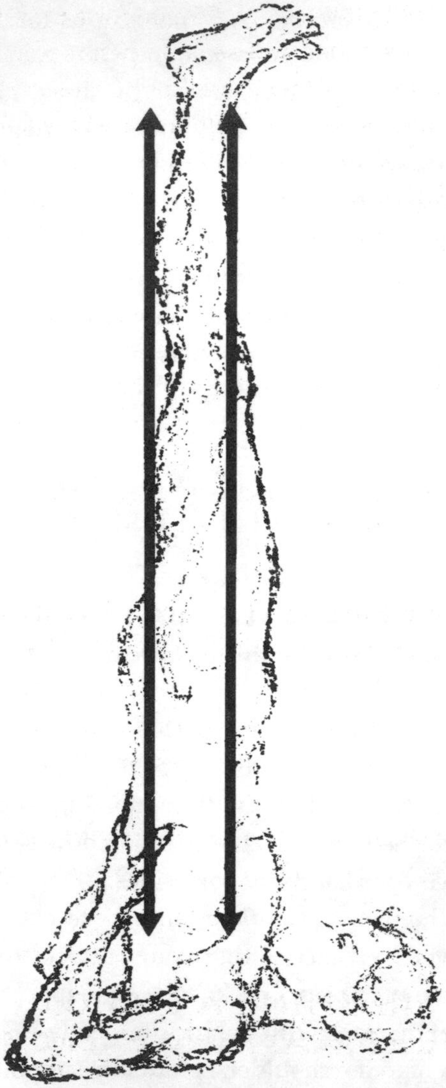

SHOULDERSTAND

As you become more sure of your balance on your shoulders, you may attempt to lift the legs. The important thing is to make sure the back is extended and straight before bringing the legs up in the air. Ultimately there should be a straight line from the feet to the shoulders, with the underside of the feet uppermost and the toes relaxed and pointing backwards. Try all the time to work the hands further up the back in the direction of the shoulders, bringing the elbows closer together. There should be minimum pressure on the upper back and shoulders – the weight should be distributed evenly throughout the body, with the spine and legs stretching and lengthening.

To come out of the posture, drop the tips of the toes back beyond the top of the head, touching the floor if possible and rounding the back gently. Now slide the legs forwards, keeping them bent, with the knees close to the face, and the hands loosely stretched beyond the top of the head. Keep the knees bent, feet in the air, and push the back of the waist down into the floor to relieve any pressure. Place the feet on the floor close to the buttocks, then clasp the hands round the back of the head and lift the head a few inches with the chin pointing down into the gap between the collar bones, and the buttocks slightly lifting. Replace the head on the floor, keeping the back of the neck extended, clasp the bent knees into the chest, then release the legs and slide them out along the floor with the toes relaxing outwards.

FINISHING A SESSION: ONE – BREATHING EXERCISES

On the most basic level the breath is essentially connected to our bodily functions. We can live for weeks without food, for days without water, yet without breathing we would be dead in minutes. Breath is quite simply our connection to life.

The specialized yoga breathing practices have multiple functions. They can create easier and less restricted access to oxygen, and more fluent expulsion of carbon dioxide. Thus they can make us feel more invigorated and keep the whole system working more effectively. And, since breathing is also intimately bound up with our nervous system, conscious control of the breath process can alter our emotional state and be a precursor to meditative practices. You only need to monitor how your breathing alters as your feelings and moods change to grasp the very subtle interaction between them.

On an even more subtle level, breath is associated with the *pranic* energy which was described above. *Prana* is the living force of the air in which we function. It follows then that breath control also affects the way in which *prana* works on our system. It has a direct link with the *nadis* – the invisible energy channels within us – and can have a forcible influence both spiritually and psychically.

The following are the simplest yoga breathing practices. They can be carried out at the end of a session, before deep relaxation. You should sit down comfortably to do them, either on the floor (on a cushion or blanket if you prefer) with legs folded, or sitting in a chair that does not permit you to go to sleep!

ALTERNATE NOSTRIL BREATHING (ANULOMA VILOMA)

Press the right thumb against the right nostril to close it gently. Breathe in through the left nostril. Bring the ring finger to the left nostril and close it too, holding the breath briefly, then release the right nostril and breathe out slowly and evenly through it while keeping the left closed. Breathe in through the right, still keeping the left nostril closed, then close both nostrils briefly before releasing the left nostril and exhaling through it. Repeat this series six times. The exercise should have a calming, harmonizing effect; do it whenever you are feeling stressed and unquiet.

HEAD-CLEARING EXERCISE (KAPALABHATI)

This is a rather forceful exercise, which has exactly the described effect. Breathe out completely through the nose and pull the abdominal area well in. As you inhale, let the abdomen relax out. Do this quickly (about two breaths per second), for up to 20 breaths, ensuring in particular that each exhalation is strong and forceful.

HUMMING BREATH (BRAHMARI)

As you breathe in through the nose, half-close the back of the throat so that you make a snoring sound. As you exhale slowly, make a humming sound by pressing the air against the back of your lips. Try to make each sound strong and even, feeling the vibration in the different areas of the mouth and head. Repeat the exercise up to ten times.

FINISHING A SESSION: TWO – DEEP RELAXATION

The best way to use this relaxation session is to read it through thoroughly so you become very familiar with it. Then make a tape of the instructions, giving yourself enough time to carry each one out. You may also like to practise it in turns with a friend, one reading the instructions to the other.

Make sure that you have something soft to lie on, although it should not be so soft that you go to sleep immediately. Often we go to sleep still full of muscular tension, as well as with our minds still churning away. This is a slow, guided process of letting go with 'awareness'. If you do sleep afterwards it will be a deeply rewarding rest.

Lie on the floor with your knees bent, your feet on the floor and your arms resting loosely on the floor beyond the top of your head. Close your eyes gently. Take a few easy breaths. Now let the legs drop until they are fully extended on the floor. Lie with the feet two to three foot apart, the toes dropping outwards. If you have any back problems you can keep the knees bent. Bring the arms down so that they are lying at a 45-degree angle from the sides of the body, the palms facing upwards. Make sure the back of the neck is extended and that the back of the head is resting on the floor.

Bring yourself into the 'here and now'. Drop any thoughts of what you have been doing, what you are going to do. Be aware of any sounds around you, from the street or garden outside, or from indoors. Become aware of what you are lying on, the feeling of the rug or carpet, the temperature of the air, the pulsation of your circulation, the rhythm of your heart.

Become aware of your toes. Wriggle them gently, contract them, then let them go. As you let go, feel any tension draining away from them and allow them to feel soft and heavy. Now bring the attention into the feet, contract them slightly then let go, feeling any tension draining away. Let the feeling of relaxation continue up into the ankles, allowing them to feel soft and heavy.

Then bring the relaxation up into the legs. Feel the points where your body is in contact with the floor – the calves, the weight of the back of the thighs. Feel those contact points becoming heavier, feel any tension points easing and releasing.

Allow yourself to become aware of the heaviness of the legs, of their weight on the floor. Now feel the buttocks resting on the floor. Feel any tension seeping out of the body. Feel the whole of the area around the pelvis relax, allow yourself to let go in the hips, deep into the lower abdomen. Allow the whole abdominal area to relax. Allow this relaxed feeling to rise up into the waist, all around the waist into the small of the back.

Now feel the sides of the torso relaxing. Feel as if the body is gently expanding, with its sides dropping further apart from each other. Feel the skin soften, the diaphragm and stomach loosen. Let the rib cage gently expand, let the lungs and heart become slow and relaxed. Feel the relaxation deep in the chest; as you breathe out let the chest feel freer and softer. Allow the whole of the back to relax. Feel each contact point as it lays on the floor; at each of these points feel the body soften and release.

Allow this feeling of expanding and releasing to fill the shoulders. Let any tension drain away, through the shoulders and the arms, out through the wrists and hands and fingers. Let the elbows relax, and the wrist joints; let the fingers gently curl. Feel the heaviness of the backs of the hands as they rest on the floor. Sigh out any remaining tension; on each out-breath imagine yourself becoming heavier and heavier.

Now feel the relaxation in your neck. Feel the softness of the skin on the neck and feel the top of the spine gently at rest. Allow this feeling of relaxation to travel all the way down the whole of the spine; trace the spine to the coccyx – the tailbone – just between the buttocks. Then travel in your imagination up the spine again, resting it even more heavily against the floor.

Let the face relax. Allow the jaw to drop open slightly, the lips to part and feel soft. Let the tongue rest behind the lower teeth. Let the cheeks relax, feel the weight of the eyeballs resting gently back in the eyesockets. Feel the scalp loosen and relax.

Feel the heavy weight of the head on the floor. Feel the easy, gentle flow of breath as it flows evenly through both nostrils. Trace the passage of the breath, down past the back of the throat, easily and gently into the lungs. Each time you breathe in, feel the whole body soften and expand. Each time you breathe out, feel yourself become more heavy and released. Allow everything to relax: skin, muscles, internal organs, nerves, bones.

Allow the mind to relax. Be aware of any thoughts, but simply watch them, noting their presence as if they are floating across the mind like clouds. Watch them come into the mind, see their shape and pattern, texture and colour. Then watch them gently slip away. Be aware of them but not affected by them. Savour this deep, relaxed state for as long as you please.

When you feel ready, start to deepen the in-breath. As you breathe in, begin to imagine you are taking fresh energy and life into the body. Still staying very relaxed, allow the energy to travel round the body, down to the toes, into the fingers, along the limbs. Feel the energy begin to move you, start to move the toes, then the fingers. Let the body come back to life, slowly bringing the feet together, stretching out. Allow yourself to stretch very gently, without disturbance. Bring the hands up beyond the top of the head, stretch all along the left side of the body, from the tips of the toes to the fingertips, then relax that side and stretch the right. Release again, and this time stretch diagonally, from the left toes up to the right fingertips. Release and reverse the stretch, from the left fingers to the right toes. Release and be aware of your gentle breathing. Keep the eyes closed.

Now curl the body over softly to the left side, like a foetus, and be aware of the beating of the heart. Then uncurl and sit up, with the eyes still closed, into a comfortable position, the spine upright and the head tilted forwards, chin towards the chest. Feel with each in-breath the energy returning to the spine and filling the whole body. Now place the palms of the hands over the eyes, open the eyes behind the hands, then take the hands away.

8

YOGA FOR CLEANSING AND PURIFYING

WAYS TO INCREASE YOUR ENERGY AND POWER

In addition to the basic practices of *hatha* yoga given in Chapter Seven, there are various additional methods of moving energy which also belong predominantly to the *hatha* system. This energy shift can have a cleansing effect in several directions. 'Cleansing' sounds vague, but the feeling it causes is specific. Clear of toxic wastes, we feel sparkling and free from aches and pains, boundlessly positive. Tireless yet well-balanced, we have a sense of lightness and freedom both physically and mentally.

We hear a lot about eating pure, cleansing foods – organic, wholemeal and largely vegetarian – which rid the body of pollutants and increase its immunity to disease. But what we find harder to recognize is the way in which we can purify our mental, spiritual and psychic systems as well. Yoga cleansing methods in fact work synchronistically. As the body becomes less burdened, thoughts will become clearer and you will find yourself spiritually recharged. The effect of painful, 'pollutant' thought patterns will become significantly less. You will also find yourself able to withstand any negative impact you may experience from people and things in your environment.

Like all of yoga, the effects are hard to measure scientifically, but easy to assess subjectively. Cleaning up your life works on all levels!

YOGA DIET

The classic yoga diet is a vegetarian, wholefood one. It's the diet that used to be considered 'cranky' – followed only by health food freaks. During the last 20 years healthy eating has come out of the closet, and what yoga practitioners have been advocating for centuries is now an acknowledged way of life. Based on vegetables, fruit, beans, wholegrains, nuts, seeds, and some dairy produce, this diet hardly needs to be reiterated. There are, however, some slight adjustments if you want to be truly yogic. Onions and garlic are considered stimulating – *rajasic* foods according to the system of the *gunas* – and used less than in a regular wholefood diet. Strong seasonings are also generally avoided. Milk and dairy produce are considered *sattvic* and therefore regarded less cautiously than the latest research into fats may warrant.

Most important for the yoga diet is the emphasis on rejecting foods which putrefy readily. Top of this list are meat and fish (unlike dairy and vegetable produce which only decay or ferment). One argument in favour of our inherent vegetarianism says that even when we eat animal produce, we go for vegetarian species rather than carnivorous ones. Thus we are consuming vital vegetable life albeit in a second-hand way. We are also reminded that our physiology is akin to that of vegetarian animals, in particular our teeth and our digestive system which seem to be better suited to processing fruit and vegetables. Another reason for not eating meat is the yoga requirement of *ahimsa* – that is, non-violence and avoiding harm to any living being. Thus many yoga practitioners are ethical vegetarians.

Yoga practitioners have always advocated avoiding processed, denaturalized foods, living instead on simple food which is as fresh and close to its natural origins as possible. The further away food is from its source, the more contaminated it becomes. Foodstuffs which have been treated more and more scientifically to make them longer lasting, not to mention attractive to a palette which no longer remembers the taste of unadulterated foodstuffs, subject the body to an increasing range of undesirable substances. As well as being simply unnecessary, these can often be hindrances to health, both addictive and allergenic.

While we are constantly indoctrinated with the idea of healthy eating, there is a strange dichotomy in that we are equally tempted by an endless supply of foods that have been tampered with in all sorts of ways. While we have the knowledge of what we should be eating, very few of us have the opportunity to put it into practice. Eating natural, wholesome food may demand rather more work than we would like, from special shopping for organic produce (or growing it yourself!) to planning meals in order to combine vegetable proteins well. These meals often need extra preparation and cooking time than that required to pop a ready-made meal in the microwave. Like disciplining yourself for yoga practice, a system of correct feeding also needs time and some effort.

It is also true that while there are basic rules, no one diet suits everybody. According to the Indian *ayurvedic* medical system, different types of people have different dietary requirements. Some may need watery, uncooked salad foods. Others benefit from warming types of food with a high carbohydrate content. Animal produce may be required at times. Macrobiotic eating, a system originating in Japan, also applies therapeutic principles to the individual. It advises you to vary the kind of foods you eat according to the temperature and the season, and also takes into account your emotional balance, your physical state and the various stages of life. The Instinctotherapy system, which originated in France, also makes some wise points. It aims to restore a natural ability to choose by instinct – mostly using the sense of smell – what will be most useful to your body from a range of pure, natural foodstuffs at each meal.

Practising yoga is a way of getting back to your true self; returning to a state of natural balance. Increasingly, it will become possible for you to assess for yourself the correct diet at any one time. As you practise, you will find yourself becoming more in tune with your own self and your own needs. This enhanced sensitivity may well help you know which foods to eat and which to avoid. You will become more in touch with yourself, aware of what you need to eat, and when. Once you start to eat more simply it will become easier for you to distinguish the foods you need instead of being confused by the unnatural combinations of prepackaged food.

Thus the principles of the yoga diet are the basic ones known to anyone interested in health: primarily vegetarian, with the emphasis on fresh, natural, unprocessed foods, simply prepared. In addition to this, however, you should aim to listen to your own body. You are the only one who really knows what you need.

FASTING

The fasting process has always been part of the practice of purification. Fasting is the most dramatic means of clearing the body of toxic wastes and has been used in natural healing for centuries for treating everything from flu to cancer. However, fasting works on more than just the physical level; it has played an important part in consciousness-altering ritual in religious and mystical practices throughout the ages and civilizations. Even if you go on a fast for purely physical reasons, it will benefit your mind. A feeling of detachment and clarity develops, and with this an overview of life and how to deal with its problems.

Anyone can fast. It is a good thing to do if you have been overeating (after Christmas is an especially strategic time!), or if you have been feeling generally out of sorts, or when you are ill. You should prepare yourself for fasting by eating less than normal for a day or two beforehand. If this is your first fast, do it only for one day. Decide whether you are going to fast on water only, or on juice or fruit. A water fast will be the most effective. Drink the water as hot as you can bear it, as much as you can take. You may add a slice of lemon to the water.

If you fast on juice, it should be extracted from fresh (preferably organic) fruit or vegetables just before you drink it. Avoid prepackaged juices. As with the hot water, sip the juice continuously. If you take fruit, avoid oranges and bananas; grapes are best. Eat as much of the fruit as you want, when you want.

To come off a fast, take a little fresh fruit for breakfast the next day. Lunch should be a light salad of vegetables only – no protein. For the evening meal – which you should take in the early evening, no later than 7 p.m.– have a light grain, such as rice, with cooked vegetables. If you fast for two or more days, the fast should be broken more slowly. Take only fruit for the first day, then salads, and only return to protein foods on the third day after the fast.

As well as carrying out a fast for a particular reason, fasting is recommended at the changes of the seasons, four times a year.

LOCKING IN YOUR ENERGY

Physical postures, in conjunction with special breathing techniques, are powerful methods for altering *pranic* energy and redistributing its flow around the body. These should not be attempted by beginners, and it is advisable to be thoroughly familiar with the simple breathing exercises outlined in Chapter Seven, and to have been practising these for at least six months before you start on these more complex breathing patterns.

In Sanskrit the posture/breath combinations are called *bandhas*. They 'lock' energy in one place, encouraging the building of energetic power and preventing it from dissipating. This energy can then be re-directed in a natural and healthy manner. Practising *bandhas* will strengthen your control over the body energy system, helping it to regenerate and circulate in a healthy way. In particular, try to become aware of what is happening internally as you practise these energy locks. Notice where the force of energy is stored, and what happens when you release it. The exercises that follow can be added to your regular practice after the simple breathing exercises (*See Finishing a Session: One*).

JALANDHARA BANDHA

Sit comfortably with the spine upright. Breathe in, then bring your chin down towards the chest, tucking it as far as possible into the little hollow between your collar bones. Close your eyes. Make sure you are not straining your neck, shoulders or face. Hold the breath for a slow count of five. As you exhale slowly, raise the head and open your eyes, trying to move in time with the breath. Take a few normal, easy breaths, then repeat *jalandhara bandha*. Do the *bandha* three times in all. Note that this position occurs naturally when you are doing the shoulderstand, so try to progress to doing the locked breath at the same time.

UDDIYANA BANDHA

Sit in a comfortable seated position, making sure the spine is upright. Place the backs of your hands on your knees, with your fingers lightly curled and relaxed. Exhale completely. Now pull your abdominal muscles up and back, creating a kind of cave underneath the lower rib cage. Hold for a count of five. As you breathe in, release the abdomen in a controlled way. Rest for a few breaths and repeat, then do the whole thing again so you practise three of these *bandhas* in total.

MOOLA BANDHA

Again, sitting in a comfortable position, with the spine upright and the hands as in *uddiyana bandha*, breathe out. Then lift the muscles of the pelvic floor so that the anus and perineum contract. Try not to contract any other muscles, such as those of the legs, arms, shoulders or face. You should feel the upward movement of energy. Hold for a count of five, then release gently as you inhale. Repeat twice, taking some easy, gentle breaths in between.

A BALANCED ATTITUDE

Another way to control the *pranic* energy is by holding certain attitudes or gestures, called *mudras* in Sanskrit. These look deceptively simple, but their purpose is to do no less than arouse the inherent spiritual forces which are said to reside in us all. Originally the practices were highly esoteric, taught only to initiates for specific purposes; they could be complex and powerful, warding off old age and delaying death. Today we have neither the personal teachers nor the time to devote to learning these secret techniques, but we can do simplified versions of them which harmonize and fine-tune the energy system. Ideally, these practices should be done when you are familiar with the system of locks explained above, and also when you are thoroughly cleansed internally by the correct diet and proper elimination of toxins.

JNANA MUDRA

Sit, preferably with your legs crossed, or otherwise in a comfortable position with your spine erect. Place your hands so that their backs are on your knees. Put the tip of your thumb and the tip of your forefinger together. Sit in this position for as long as you feel comfortable, with eyes closed. Make sure your breathing is gentle and relaxed, and that all parts of your body are as relaxed as they can be while still maintaining your upright position. This posture may seem simple; try to be aware of the subtle energy flow between the fingers and the thumbs. You may be able to feel some warmth or tingling and also become aware of the upsurge in the circulation of energy throughout the body.

DHAYANA MUDRA

Sit in a cross-legged or comfortable seated position. In your lap, hold the back of your left hand in the palm of your right hand, with the thumbs just touching one another. Again, close the eyes gently, breathe softly and become aware of the containment and balancing of the energy.

MAHA MUDRA

Sitting on the floor, stretch the right leg out straight and bend the left so that the heel of the left foot is against the right groin. Now stretch so that your hands reach as far down the right leg as possible, keeping the leg straight. Breathe in. Drop the chin to the chest as in *jalandhara bandha*. Now pull in the abdomen, as in *uddiyana bandha*. Pull in the anal and genital muscles, as in *moola bandha*. Close your eyes and hold the breath for a count of five. You can increase the count gradually as you become familiar with the posture. Breathe out slowly and carefully. Release the posture. Repeat, this time stretching out the left leg.

A CLEAN SWEEP

These time-honoured yoga practices (*kriyas* in Sanskrit) wash the body internally. The first is quite simple, the others may require the help of a qualified yoga teacher to explain exactly what to do.

NETI

Ideally this should be practised each morning. It is also very useful when you have a cold or if you feel a cold coming on. You will need to obtain a small jug, or an invalid feeding cup (obtainable from chemists). Fill it with fresh, clean, lukewarm water, with a pinch of salt dissolved in it. Tilt the head on one side and slightly backwards, and pour a little water at a time into the uppermost nostril, sniffing it up to make sure it enters the whole of the nostril. The water should go all the way along the nasal passageway, and will run down the back of the throat. When one nostril is thoroughly cleansed, wash the other. The process may be uncomfortable at first, especially in the sinuses.

Persevere if you can. You will find it becomes easy in time, clearing the head and making you less susceptible to colds.

NAULI

This exercise helps clear the intestines. Stand with your legs slightly apart, and your knees bent. Rest your hands on your thighs. Exhale completely. Now draw the abdomen in, as in *uddiyana bandha*. Now try to isolate and push out the central muscle, which runs downwards from just below the centre of the rib cage to the pubis. Once you have managed to make the muscle stand out, try moving it from left to right. Initially you can do this by physically pushing it down with each hand so that it moves to the other side. This exercise will perform a powerful massage to the internal organs.

DHAUTI

This exercise is unlikely to be welcomed with much enthusiasm by modern practitioners, but it is one of the classics of yoga cleansing practices and still has its adherents. First thing in the morning, on an empty stomach, take a clean bandage and swallow a small portion of it while holding onto the other end. Then pull it out carefully. The aim is to swallow about 15 feet of bandage, drawing waste accumulations out with it! After the practice you should take a glass of warm water.

BASTI

Again, this exercise is not likely to be very popular nowadays but it is another classic yoga practice, which works similarly to an enema. You will need six inches of clean flexible tubing, half an inch in diameter. Squat in some clean warm water up to the navel. Insert the tube a little way into the anus. Holding onto the tube, draw water up through the anus and then expel it.

BREATHING DEEPER

These more advanced breathing practices have profound effects on the *pranic* energy flow, and consequently on the mind and spirit. Do these only if you have mastered the previous breathing practices, as and when required. Usually they are done at the end of a practice session, prior to deep relaxation. However you may do a breathing session on its own, starting with the simpler practices and progressing into the more powerful ones that follow here. You should be sitting in a comfortable cross-legged or kneeling position to do the breathing practices.

UJJAYI

Inhale fully, closing the back of the throat slightly as in *brahmari* (*see Chapter Seven*). Now hold the breath, and do *jalandhara bandha* (chin into the chest) and *moola bandha* (pulling up the pelvic floor). Release these locks, and place the right thumb over the right nostril as you exhale smoothly through the left nostril. Repeat, closing the left nostril with the left thumb on the exhalation. Do four rounds altogether, increasing gradually to ten.

SURYA BHEDA

Close the left nostril with the third and little fingers of your right hand, and breathe in through the right nostril. Hold your breath and practise *jalandhara bandha*. Release the lock, close your right nostril with your right thumb, release the left nostril and exhale through it. Repeat, breathing in through the left nostril, holding *jalandhara bandha* and exhaling through the right as you close off the left with the two fingers. Repeat and gradually increase.

BHASTRIKA

This is the 'bellows' breath. It is an extremely powerful energy-raiser. Breathe out completely and pull in the abdominal muscles, as in *kapalabhati* (*see Chapter Seven*). Now close both nostrils with fingers and thumb, and do *jalandara bandha* (chin to chest) and *moola bandha* (lifting the pelvic floor), while holding the breath. Now partially release the right nostril, and exhale and inhale forcibly through it, keeping the left nostril closed. Inhale and exhale between four to eight times, ending with a firm exhalation. Then close the right nostril and partially open the left. Breathe in and out through it the same number of times you did with the right. Do not take in any air through the mouth or the closed nostril. Make sure that the body does not become tense and that the breaths, although strong, are easy and unforced.

YOGA SPECIFICS

Yoga has answers for many common problems. Here, briefly, are some of them. If you have any long-term health problems, you are strongly recommended to contact a qualified yoga teacher for yoga therapy (*see Resource Guide*).

Asthma: Relaxation. Triangle. Cobra. Shoulderstand. Breathing exercises, both simple and deeper.

Back pain: Forward bend. Deep relaxation.

Blood pressure (high): Forward bend. Shoulderstand.

Blood pressure (low): Hero pose. Shoulderstand (regulates blood flow).

Colds: Neti. Alternate nostril breathing. Lion (Kneel on the floor with your hands palms down on the floor in front of you. On a forceful exhalation, stick your tongue out and thrust your face forwards. Breathe in, bringing the body back as it was, and repeat four times).

Constipation: Kapalabhati. Uddiyana bandha. Nauli.

Depression: Cat. Simple breathing exercises. Deep breathing exercises.

Diarrhoea: Relaxation. Shoulderstand.

Digestive problems: Cat. Cobra. Uddiyana bandha.

Headache: Slow warm-ups, including bending from the waist and slow uncurling to standing position. Starting session relaxation. Finishing session deep relaxation.

Painful periods: Cobbler. Forward bend. Cobra. Relaxation. Meditation.

Premenstrual tension; menopause: Cobbler.

Rheumatism and arthritis: Starting session warming up. Kapalabhati.

Stress: Relaxation exercises. Starting session warming up. Cat. Meditations.

Varicose veins: Shoulderstand.

9

RESOURCE GUIDE

ADDRESSES

Astanga Vinyasa Yoga
12 Beatty Avenue
Coldean
Brighton
East Sussex BN1 9ED
Tel: 01273 687071

British Wheel of Yoga
1 Hamilton Place
Boston Road
Sleaford
Lincs NG34 7ES
Tel: 01529 306851

Himalayan International Institute
70 Claremont Road
London W13 0DG
Tel: 0181 991 8090

Iyengar Yoga
Maida Vale Yoga Institute
223a Randolph Avenue
London W9 1NL
Tel: 0171 624 3080

Sivananda Yoga Centre
51 Felsham Road
London SW15 1AZ
Tel: 0181 780 0160

Yoga Biomedical Trust
PO Box 140
Cambridge CB4 3SY
Tel: 01223 67301

Yoga Centre
Church Farm House
Spring Close Lane
Cheam
Surrey SM3 8PU
Tel: 0181 644 0309

Yoga for Health Foundation
Ickwell Bury
Northill
Near Biggleswade
Bedfordshire SG18 9EF
Tel: 01767 627271

International Yoga Teachers' Association
c/o Shirley Deffert
15 Tarrow Close
Hornsby
2077 New South Wales
Australia

Ananda
14618 Tyler Foote Road
Nevada City
California 95959
USA
Tel: 916 292 3462

Omega Institute
260 Lake Drive
Rhinebeck
NY 12572
USA
Tel: 800 944 1001 or 914 266 4444

Unity and Yoga Association
4601 East Euclid Avenue
Phoenix
Arizona
USA